BIBLE
MASTERY
SERIES
BMS

ROMANS:
Let Justice Roll Down

Jim Townsend

DAVID C. COOK PUBLISHING CO.
ELGIN, ILLINOIS • WESTON, ONTARIO

To Professor Zane Hodges—
an individual with both integrity
and ingenious insights

Romans: Let Justice Roll Down
© 1988 by David C. Cook Publishing Co.

David C. Cook Publishing Co., 850 North Grove Avenue, Elgin, IL 60120. Printed in U.S.A.

Editor: Gary Wilde
Designer: Dawn Lauck
Cover: Bakstad Photographics
Cartoonist: Chuck Asay

ISBN: 1-55513-231-6
Library of Congress Catalog Number: 88-70104

CONTENTS

INTRODUCTION

Welcome to the Bible Mastery Series, designed to aid serious Bible students in group settings. Ideally, every student should have a copy of this study manual. Then the group sessions will be spent focusing largely upon the questions and activities at the back of the book in the DIRECTIONS FOR GROUP LEADERS section, p. 113. **Since all participants should have read the up-front commentary before class, the group's time can be spent primarily upon sharing experiences about how to apply these truths to their lives (rather than in factual and interpretive discussions).**

Each chapter contains many quotes and ideas from the best of past and present evangelical scholarship. In effect, I have provided a mini-library of information from the standard, solid commentators that Bible students will turn to for interpretation and explanation. In most cases, the Notes section at the back of the book will give sources for the information. I did the digging, you get the results!

The Symbols

Various boxes are set off from the rest of the text. These will give background information or illustrations from such areas as theology, archaeology, original languages, etc. Here is a key to the symbols:

 GREEKSPEAK: Concise explanations of important Greek words, tenses, syntax, to help with interpreting the text's meaning.

 THEOLOGITALK: Discusses theological terms and doctrinal issues in relation to the text.

CAN YOU DIG IT? Gives valuable cultural insight from archaeology.

QUOTABLE QUOTES: Memorable statements from various sources.

 WINDOW ON THE WORD: Anecdotal material to illustrate a point in the text.

THOUGHT QUESTION: A chance to pause and reflect on issues raised in the text.

Romans: A Universal Drama

A judge's job is to *justify* (that is, pronounce okay or "not guilty") the just person. God is Supreme Court Justice of the universe. The Book of Romans is about that universal courtroom drama—and its dilemma. How can God—a just judge—let any of us off of the hook, since we're all guilty of sinning (Rom. 3:23)? Is God the ultimate unjust judge?

No. The Book of Romans unfolds how human beings can be justified. Chapters 1—8 zero in on the unfolding of *justification*—how those who are guilty can be pronounced "not guilty."

Not only are sinning humans unjust, but God appears to be unjust in what He is doing: 1) in justifying the unjust (Rom. 4:5); and 2) in (seemingly) invalidating His promises to the Jewish nation. Therefore, Romans 9—11 answers the question: Can God's seemingly unjust actions be justified (that is, vindicated)?

Finally, how do people made right (or justified) with God actually act? That is the subject of Romans 12—16. A righteous acquittal of the unrighteous should ultimately result in their righteous actions. These actions are not relegated to wispy theory, but can be nailed down in form of the way the righteous relate: 1) to civil government (chap. 13); 2) to relevant relative issues (chaps. 14 and 15); and 3) to real-life relationships (chap. 16).

Welcome to the portals of the magnificent cathedral of Romans!

CHAPTER
1

BAD NEWS, GOOD NEWS
Romans 1

Chiropractors claim to be realigners, straighteners. Nerves extend from the vertebrae in the human backbone. If those vertebrae get out of line or twisted, the various nerves can be pinched, causing pain and shutting off proper nerve functions to areas where they send their impulses.

Chiropractic theory says that out-of-kilter vertebrae need to be put back in place. These vertebrae will not adjust properly on their own. Rather, they require external readjusting. Whether or not one favors chiropractors, the skill provides an excellent Biblical illustration. In Romans, God is the great Chiropractor. God specializes in taking what has been made crooked, misshapen, and out of line because of sin and putting them back into right relationship. God is the great Rightener.

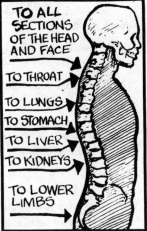

TO ALL SECTIONS OF THE HEAD AND FACE

TO THROAT

TO LUNGS

TO STOMACH

TO LIVER

TO KIDNEYS

TO LOWER LIMBS

Sin is crookedness, but God has perfectly straight standards. All humans are crooked to one degree or another (Rom. 3:23). We need (as the old highway signs would say) to "get right with God." But we can no more accomplish that on our own than I can step outside of my skin to push several out-of-line vertebrae between my shoulder blades back into alignment. I need an outside Specialist. Therefore, God the Chiropractor enters the picture.

Romans is all about rightness with God (and humans, too). Right, righteousness, just, justification—these concepts are central to Romans. Many Jews believed Paul was not right about what he said about how to be right with God. Partially to answer the flak he got, Paul presented this complex problem's answer by writing Romans. Romans may be outlined:

I. *The Theological Problem—how can a person be right with God? (Rom. 1—8);*

II. *The National Problem—how does Israel fit into this (seemingly new) scheme of justification? And is God acting justly with Israel? (Rom. 9—11);*

III. *The Social Problem—how is this rightness with God worked out in relationships? (Rom. 12—16).*

" Classical scholar Alexander Souter called Paul's Epistles "the most valuable writings in the world."
— *The Earliest Latin Commentaries on the Epistles of St. Paul*

Ernst Kasemann called Romans "the most important theological Epistle in Christian history." — *Commentary on Romans*

Grace Seminary president Alva McClain called Romans "the greatest book in the Bible." — *Romans*

Samuel Taylor Coleridge called Romans "the most profound writing extant."

Martin Luther said: "This epistle is . . . the most important document in the New Testament, the gospel in its purest expression."

Merrill Tenney claimed that Romans has given "a fuller and more systematic view of the heart of Christianity than any other of Paul's epistles, with the possible exception of Ephesians."
— *New Testament Survey*

Romans 1—8 deals with:
A. the need for justification—or universal sin (Rom. 1:1—3:20);
B. the nature of justification (Rom. 3:21—4:25);
C. the results of justification (Rom. 5:1-11; 6:1—8:39);
D. the relationship between sin and justification (Rom. 5:12-21).

Obviously, the heart and soul of this section is the word "justification." The business of a judge is to "justify the righteous, and condemn the wicked" (Deut. 25:1, KJV). A just judge must seek to pronounce the just to be all right, but not to acquit, justify, or pronounce "not guilty" the unrighteous who have violated society's right standards. In classical Greek . . . *dikaios* "just," or "right" was used as an adjective to describe a wagon, a horse, or something else to indicate that it was fit for its intended use.[1] We might size up such a wagon by saying: "It's okay" or "it's alright" (it meets the standards).

At the outset of Romans, however, we are assaulted by the fact that humanity is not "okay" with God. But the good news of Romans is: "I'm not okay. You're not okay. But that's still okay, because God has made a way for us to be okay in Christ."

Paul hadn't been to Rome. Therefore, in Romans 1:1-7 he established that these nonvisited Romans fell under his jurisdiction. The stairstep logic runs as diagrammed below.

STAIRSTEPS OF LOGIC IN ROMANS 1:1-7

```
                                                        PAUL
                                                        (vs. 1)
                                              GOSPEL
                                              (vs. 1)
                                    CHRIST
                                    (vss. 3, 4)
                          APOSTLE
                          (vs. 5)
              GENTILES
              (vs. 5)
ROMANS
(vs. 6)
```

Paul's whole mental horizon was the *Gospel,* and the Gospel's ball-bearing was *Christ* (vss. 3, 4). It was "through him [i.e., Christ]" (vs. 5) that Paul became an *apostle.* Since he was an apostle to the *Gentiles,* and since *Romans* fell into the category of being Gentiles, Paul had jurisdiction over them as their apostle.

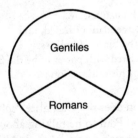

Paul's Mental Horizon (Rom. 1:1-7)

J. Agar Beet said, "Paul's opening sentence is a crystal arch spanning the gulf between the Jew of Tarsus and the Christians at Rome."[2] Of all Paul's opening sentences in his letters this is the longest—perhaps because he was writing to a group he'd never visited. The first sentence does not end until after verse 7 in the King James Version.

Ω In Romans 1:1 Paul spoke of himself as "set apart for the gospel of God." The basic Greek word (*aphorismenos*) behind "set apart" is one from which we get our English word "horizon." It was as if, to use an illustration from Donald Grey Barnhouse, Paul had climbed up to the pinnacle of the crow's nest of a ship. As far as Paul's eye could see, as he scanned life's horizon, he saw "Gospel."

The Good News about Jesus Christ was Paul's mental horizon and magnificent obsession.

This Good News Paul proclaimed was not some novelty trinket, some trivial pursuit espoused by a huckster of ideas. Rather, as the parenthesis of verse 2 indicates, Paul's life-message was anchored to the Old Testament—it was channeled through the prophets and contained in bud form in the Jewish Scriptures.

The ball-bearing upon which that gospel pivoted is stated in verses 3 and 4. Notice the parallelism: "regarding his Son,

> who as to his human nature
>   was a descendant of David, and
> who through the Spirit of holiness
>   was declared with power to be the Son of God
>   by his resurrection . . . ."

The King James Version does not capitalize "spirit" in verse 4, so the KJV may have understood Paul to be talking about Christ's divine nature, paralleling "his human nature" (vs. 3, NIV). This makes good sense since the Holy Spirit is never elsewhere in Scripture given the exact title "Spirit of Holiness."

While Christ was the Son of God during His earthly career, He was "declared to be the Son of God with power" in His exalted condition—by means of His resurrection. The resurrection acted as His loudspeaker, broadcasting His true identity.

Jews ordinarily greeted one another with "peace" (*shalom*), and Greeks greeted friends with *chairein (KAI-rain)*. Paul Christianized *chairein*, meaning (literally) "rejoice" (Jas. 1:1), into *charis (KAH-ris)*, meaning "grace." Hence, Paul gathered up the best of both worlds—Jew and Gentile—and altered them with the chemistry of God's grace.

Paul's Unanswered Prayer (Rom. 1:8-13)

In verses 1-7 Paul established an official position in regard to the Roman church, whereas in verses 8-15 he established an intimate relationship with the same group.[3]

Surely Paul would make an excellent master model for one's prayer life. Yet in verses 8-13 Paul has a long-standing prayer registered with God that was as yet unanswered! Paul prayed persistently (vs. 9). Like a person with a nagging, chronic cough, Paul regularly made requests for his Roman readers (that is the idea behind "constantly," vs. 9). Furthermore, Paul prayed planningly (vs. 10). While some Christians act like there is something wrong with hardheaded, rational planning, Paul didn't.

? In your mind, how do praying and planning interlock? How do human desire and divine design intersect each other in Romans 1:8-13?

Paul prayed purposefully (vss. 11-13). His purposes can be charted.

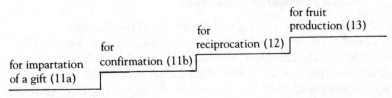

for impartation of a gift (11a) — for confirmation (11b) — for reciprocation (12) — for fruit production (13)

Can you imagine many modern pastors feeling the sentiments of Romans 1:12 about lay people? What does this show you about Paul?

Paul's I.O.U. (Rom. 1:14-17)

The one who wrote in the same letter, "Let no debt remain outstanding" (13:8), also wrote, "I am debtor" (1:14, KJV). This section might be called Paul's I.O.U.

In the 1700's, David Garrick, England's greatest actor, said he would give a hundred guineas if he could say the word "oh" as movingly as the evangelist George Whitefield (pronounced WHIT-field). The reason for Whitefield's eloquence was the same as Paul's. He possessed unbendable, heartfelt convictions. He said, "So, as much as in me is, I am ready to preach the gospel to you that are at Rome also" (vs. 15, KJV).

Romans 1:16, 17—the theme text for the letter—is peppered with Old Testament ideas. This can be seen from the chart below (adapted from John Murray):

ROM. 1:16, 17	PS. 98:1, 2
"the power of God"	"his right hand" and "arm"
"salvation"	"salvation"
"revealed"	"revealed"
"righteousness of God"	"his righteousness"

God's Good News is the power of God released and resulting in salvation (vs. 16).

TRANSFORMING POWER
Ernest Gordon told of a Christian named Fegan who asked Charles Darwin if he could use his reading room to hold Christian services. Darwin is said to have replied, "You have done more for the village in a few months than all our efforts for many years. We have never been able to reclaim a drunkard but through your services. I do not know that there is a drunkard left in the village."[4]

Although Paul was considered the apostle to the Gentiles, it appeared to be his studied tactic in evangelizing cities to aim "first for the Jew" (1:16). This "first" was one of historical precedence and not of exclusive preference. Michael Green observed that the Gospel is about a Jew preached by Jews first to Jews.[5] The term "Greek" in verse

16 means more than just people living in Greece, it includes the Greek-speaking world of Gentiles.

In the Good News God's righteousness is revealed "from faith to faith" (vs. 17, KJV). This last expression is interpreted by:

John Calvin: from one degree of faith to another;
Charles Hodge: by faith alone;
C. H. Dodd: by faith from start to finish;
T. F. Torrance: from God's faithfulness to human faith;
Donald G. Barnhouse: transmitted from one's believer's faith to the faith-response of another person.

The expression undoubtedly parallels "everyone who believes" in verse 16. Paul's theme-text is announced in Romans 1:17—"The righteous will live by faith." It is a quote from Habakkuk 2:4.

Habakkuk is the grandfather of the Protestant Reformation. Habakkuk would see the conquering Chaldeans haughtily bulldozing over his country, yet (God told him), "the righteous will live by his faith" (Hab. 2:4). That verse virtually became Paul's life-text. It is quoted in Romans 1:17; Galatians 3:11; and Hebrews 10:38. If Habakkuk fathered Paul spiritually, he became spiritual grandfather of Martin Luther. In the 1500's the tortured monk found Romans 1:17 to be for him the gate to paradise. In the 1700's another troubled soul, John Wesley, went grudgingly to a Moravian meeting in Aldersgate Street where he heard Luther's commentary on Romans being read. There Wesley's "heart was strangely warmed." He "did trust in Christ . . . alone." Therefore, the Wesleyan Awakening that altered England was the great grandchild of Habakkuk. No wonder Lewis Johnson could say, "The truth of the clause in Rom. 1:17 has had as profound an effect upon the history of the West as the Magna Charta or the Declaration of Independence."[6] Thus Paul said that "in the gospel a righteousness from God is revealed" (Rom. 1:17). This revelation of Good News (1:17) is because of a prior revelation of bad news (1:18).

1:17 ROMANS -- TWO REVELATIONS 1:18

RIGHTEOUSNESS   WRATH

"IN THE GOSPEL A RIGHTEOUSNESS FROM GOD IS REVEALED."   "THE WRATH OF GOD IS BEING REVEALED FROM HEAVEN."

A fire in a house may warm the house in the hearth, or burn the house down if unleashed. If electricity is harnessed, it will service our appliances; if connected with our wet hands, it may electrocute us. God's righteousness is like fire and electricity. God's wrath (Rom. 1:18) is His righteous revulsion against sin. Romans 1:18—3:20 informs us why this righteous "wrath of God is being revealed" (1:18). In short, it is because "all have sinned" (3:23).

God's Braille (Rom. 1:18—20)

J. H. Barrows commented, "The Himalayas are the raised letters upon which we blind children put our fingers to spell out the name of God."[7] Barrows was getting at the idea that nature teaches human beings something about God, but "their minds were blinded" (II Cor. 3:14, KJB; cf. 4:4) by sin. Therefore, the human race is like a blind man feeling his way by cane along a treacherous path. God, to some extent, is legible in the book of nature, but only in a limited way. Christian theologians speak of this as natural revelation. As someone once said, "In nature we see God's fingerprints . . . but what we sinners need to see is Christ's nailprints."[8]

What "truth" (Rom. 1:18) the created being has is, as it were, held down in a box with the possessor trying to sit on the lid. But while in their sinfulness humans are diking back the truth against themselves, God's great reservoir of justice is rising and will someday have to be unleashed upon that buildup of sin. "The wrath of God is being revealed from heaven against all the godlessness" (Rom. 1:18). Charles Williams once commented that if God has moral character and humans have moral choice, then we have to assume the possibility of a hell. While the term "hell" is never found in Paul's writings, "wrath" is part of Paul's stock vocabulary (Rom. 1:18; Eph. 2:3; Col. 3:6; I Thess. 1:10). Whenever humanity flaunts God in unholiness, its defying sword blade meets that whirring, buzzing wheel of holiness from which, as it were, sparks of wrath must invariably fly. As J. B. Phillips put it, "God is . . . against . . . godlessness" (Rom. 1:18).

Like "Friday," the Indian on the island in Robinson Crusoe's story, God has left discernible tracks of His presence in the created order. "What may be known about God" from nature "is plain to them, because God has made it plain to them" (Rom. 1:19).

The problem is that we sin-blinded creatures, in another sense, all too clearly see. Paul plays upon this point in verse 20. The "invisible" (or unseen) attributes of God have been "clearly seen" (1:20). What is decipherable by human beings is that there is a Supreme Being. Like

14

blind people trying to decipher Egyptian hieroglyphics, however, they are still left basically in the dark. Without the Christian Gospel, which is "the power of God" resulting in salvation (1:16), the callous non-Christian only senses the "eternal power and divine nature" (vs. 20) of this great Existent One. Instead of being aligned with God's favor, he is left "without excuse" (vs. 20). Therefore, it is precisely because "the wrath of God is being revealed" against all sin (vs. 18) that sinners need "a righteousness from God . . . revealed" (vs. 17) and provided in the Gospel.

Abandoned Mind Shafts (Rom. 1:21-28)

In *The Brothers Karamazov*, Boris Pasternak has Ivan say, "If God is not, everything is permitted." In other words: if Heaven is excluded from impinging upon human experience, all hell will break loose.

 If you go against the grain of the universe, you get splinters.
—H. H. Farmer, in Addison Leitch, *Christianity Today*

Romans 1:21-28 traces the downward spiral of those who are going against the grain of God's universe. In their minds they have abandoned God. Therefore,

> "God gave them over . . .
>   to sexual impurity" (1:24);
> "God gave them over
>   to shameful lusts" (1:26);
> "God . . . gave them over
>   to a depraved mind" (1:28).

Because they refused God's grace, they were abandoned to wallow in their own disgrace.

Verse 21 elaborates upon verse 18. These truth-suppressors hold down the truth by their unrighteous desires. As the Living Bible paraphrases: "Yes, they knew about him all right," but "they have refused to honour him as God, or to render him thanks" (NEB).

THANKING WHOM?
Katherine Mansfield's exclamation, when speaking of her delight in a lovely spot in the Alps, was, "If only one could make some small grasshoppery sound of praise to someone, of thanks to someone—but to who?" The Christian has someone to thank.

The non-Christian Nietzsche once said, "We receive but do not ask where it came from."   —John Baillie, *The Sense of the Presence of God*

15

As we descend into the cavern of their "mind shafts," so to speak, we hear the awful announcement of abandonment three times— "God . . . gave them" up (vss. 24, 26, 28). While they looked at themselves in the mirror and thought, "wise," God sized them up as "fools" (vs. 22). R. A. Torrey called them "foolosophers." The master historian Will Durant conceded, "Perhaps they too [the primitive "naked nations"] were once civilized and desisted from it as a nuisance."[9] In commenting upon Romans 1:23, Ray Stedman observed our obsession with some of our modern idols—Cougars, Mustangs, Jaguars, Cobras, etc.[10] The Living Bible paraphrases verse 24: "So God let them go ahead into every sort of sex sin, and do whatever they wanted to." God was forced to abandon them to their ways.

A Searing Catalog (Rom. 1:29-32)

Donald Grey Barnhouse claimed that the searing catalog in verses 29-31 "is the most formidable list of sins to be found in the Word of God" (Man's Ruin, p. 284). Other similar lists are found in I Corinthians 5:10, 11; II Corinthians 12:20, 21; and Galatians 5:19-21.

The word "unrighteousness" (vs. 29) may be an umbrella term, covering all the other twenty-two items found in verses 29-31. These are just the sort of sins that were the local fare at Corinth, the probable location from which Paul wrote his Letter to the Romans.

Ω   Two terms in this long list (vs. 29) are called by the technical name paronomasia (check your dictionary for meaning). A play on words is made by the similarity in sound in the Greek words *pthonos* ("envy") and *phonos* ("murder"). Noting that the only difference in pronunciation is a th, Barnhouse observed, "There is but a breath between envy and murder. Murder follows envy not only in our list but also in life."[11] The murderer is often one who has carried out "envy" to its ultimate consequence—getting rid of the person who possesses what he or she wants.

These sins protrude like porcupine quills. The NIV renders the last three in verse 29 as "strife, deceit, and malice." Such people are a walking hotbed of irritation and irritableness.

Another word where the sound is prominent in the pronunciation of the Greek word is *psithuristas*, "whisperers" (vs. 29, KJV). One can almost hear the hissing of the old serpent in that term of malicious rumormongering. "Gossips" (vs. 29) and "slanderers" (vs. 30) are malicious twins. J. B. Phillips observed that whispering gossips are "stabbers in the back." They are the secretive, polluting slanderers who dump poison into the stream of society.

16

Bible translators are divided in verse 30 between "haters of God" and "hateful to God." These people are Edisons of evil, "inventors of evil things" (vs. 30, KJV), perverting their God-given creativity for degenerate purposes. Like the Nazi concentration camp leaders, they invent inhumane cruelties. J. B. Phillips says "their minds teemed with diabolical invention" (vs. 30).

Three of the sins spotlighted in verse 30 accent arrogance ("insolent, arrogant and boastful"). Here are those who are insolent toward God and insulting to humanity. They jack themselves up by looking down on others.

Ω Another play on words is found in the Greek sound of "senseless" (*asunetous*) and "faithless" (*asunthetous*) in verse 31. In the Greek language the last four characteristics all begin with the English equivalent of "un-" (or "no"). The NIV captures this flavor by the ending "-less"—"senseless, faithless, heartless, ruthless." These people really are far "less" than God intended them to be. They are worthy of the philosopher Schopenhauer's indictment—"little inferior to the tiger and hyena in cruelty and savagery."

? Can you illustrate at least six of the 22 sins in Romans 1:29-31, showing how they crop up in some of their less overt forms in things we do?

Like those who are sitting in a theater and clapping for some cruel comedy, "they not only continued their own practices, but did not hesitate to give their thorough approval to others who did the same" (vs. 32, J. B. Phillips). "Their sin had reached a point where they received a vicarious satisfaction in the sinful deeds of others."[12] The verdict of the Supreme Court Judge upon such people is they "deserve death" (vs. 32).

CHAPTER
2
SITTING UNPRETTY
Romans 2:1—3:9

A Bloomington, Indiana, church preaches that it's a sin to watch TV. Yet one woman in the church has been a circuit board inspector in the Bloomington RCA plant—which produces televisions—for over 22 years. In fact, more people from that particular branch of churches work for RCA than for any other company in the city.

A preacher known as "John 3:16 Cook" was arrested for drunk driving in St. Petersburg, Florida. His 1975 El Dorado Cadillac plowed through two service stations and mowed down five gas pumps, barely missing hitting someone. Asked how this incident would affect his ministry, he answered, "I'll always be in God's business."[1]

A "60 Minutes" program of some years ago reviewed what groups were not paying back student loans. At that time the profession most guilty of not repaying what they had borrowed for college was lawyers—those sworn to uphold our laws!

The three illustrations cited above all reveal glaring inconsistencies between presentation and practice. Human sin is always most apparent when there is a great gulf between our reputation and reality. Romans 2 opens with an exposé of this hypocrisy.

In Romans 1:18—3:20 Paul sketched humanity's condemnation in broad brushstrokes. There appear to be three focal points:

(1) condemnation of the immoral Gentile (1:18-32);
(2) condemnation of the moral censor (2:1-15);
(3) condemnation of the hypocritical Jew (2:17—3:20).

Romans 2:1-16 can be outlined:
(1) the unprejudiced divine judgment (2:1-11); and
(2) the universal moral conscience (2:12-16).

The Censor Is Censored (Rom. 2:1-16)

It is always helpful to ask: What is "therefore" there for? When we stumble on a "therefore," we need to recheck what comes before it (2:1). Since Paul has concluded that the typically self-indulgent, down-swirling Gentile is "without excuse" (1:20) in Romans 1:18-32, he also rings his judgelike gavel on the judge of that same sinning Gentile in 2:1. "You, therefore, have no excuse."

Note the switch from "they" (e.g., 1:21, 28, 32) to "you" in 2:1. Actually the subject "you" appears five times in 2:1. One gets the impression that Paul, like Nathan before guilty David (II Sam. 12:7), is finger pointing. The interesting item in 2:1 is that the capable critic ("you who pass judgment") is condemned by his own criticism. The very fact that he can use his critical powers like a moral x-ray machine constitutes his own sentence of guilt. He can judge ("judge" or "judgment" appears three times in vs. 1); therefore, he stands self-judged. Paul's unwritten syllogism in Romans 2:1 is:

You condemn others.
You do the same things you condemn.
Therefore, you stand self-condemned.

"Gotcha!" Paul says. Just as Paul had concluded that immorally acting people were "without excuse" (1:20), so also he concludes here that their moral censors equally have "no excuse" (2:1).

CONDEMNER CONDEMNED

The classic critic sized up an owl perched in a taxidermist's window for his friends standing with him. The critic blasted the taxidermist: "If I couldn't stuff an owl better than that, I'd quit. The head is awkward, the body-poise isn't right, the feathers are terrible." His friends were rather impressed by the critic's assessment until the owl in the window turned his head and winked.[2]

A boy was arraigned before juvenile court for stealing a watermelon. After finding the boy guilty, the judge asked, "Is there anything you wish to say before I pass sentence?" The boy thoughtfully responded, "Judge, have you ever stolen a watermelon?" After a moment's electrifying silence, the judge blurted out, "Case dismissed!"[3] The essence of Romans 2:1-4 is: "you who pass judgment on someone else" (2:1) "do you think you will escape God's judgment" (2:3)? Such critics "show contempt" (2:4) for God's patience, while they "are storing up" (2:5) God's wrath. Visualize the reservoir rising!

Although the NIV breaks up Romans 2:5-10 into five sentences, in Greek it is only one sentence of 87 words. (That's a mouthful!) How terrifying a thought—to be a capitalist, ("storing up," 2:5) a spiritual Scrooge of God's wrath. It is the most tragic treasure a person could accumulate.

 A LIFETIME'S GEOLOGY

Beds of sandstone rocks, thousands of feet thick, are the sediment dropped from vanished seas, or borne down by long dried-up rivers. The chalk cliffs of Dover are the skeletons of millions upon millions of tiny organisms, and our little lives are built up by the recurrence of transient deeds.[4]

Many Protestants have been discombobulated by Romans 2:7. On the surface it seems to allow for a salvation by works. F. F. Bruce penned, "While salvation in the Bible is according to grace, judgment is always according to works."[5] Ralph Martin indicated, "No salvation by good living is taught here, but Paul is stating the principle at the heart of Jesus' teaching (Mt. 7:16-20), just as his earlier verse picks up the Lord's condemnation of a censorious and a critical spirit (v. 3; Mt. 7:1 ff.)."[6] Perhaps Cornelius the centurion (in Acts 10 and 11) is the classic New Testament case of one who "by persistence in doing good" (Rom. 2:7) sought "glory, honor and immortality" and so was granted "eternal life" (2:7; see Acts 11:14). It was not that God rewarded

Cornelius with eternal life because of his meritorious accumulation of good works. Rather, God honored the principle that "he rewards those who earnestly seek him" (Heb. 11:6). God is the great Unprejudiced One (Rom. 2:11).

Romans 2:11-15 is couched in the form of a chiasm (*chi*, pronounced *kai*, is a Greek letter like an X). A chiasm is a crossing pattern of A-B-B-A.

A	B
Gentiles	Jews
(2:12a)	(2:13)
B	A
Jews	Gentiles
(2:12b)	(2:14, 15)

> The law is not a talisman calculated to preserve those who possess it.
> —C. K. Barrett, *Romans*

The great Greek philosopher Aristotle had said: "So will the tasteful gentleman conduct himself, and be, as it were, a law to himself." Similarly, in Romans 2:14 and 15 Paul says that when Gentiles, who never possessed the written Mosaic Law, instinctively practiced the moral standards encapsuled in God's absolute Law, "they are a law for themselves" (2:14).

In the imaginary courtroom of a Gentile's heart, the conscience donned the white wig, picked up the gavel, and functioned as judge. It is as if inside our heads an invisible Clarence Darrow and William Jennings Bryan are wielding words against each other—accusing or excusing us.

Conscience (2:15) is "a word not [ever] found in the Old Testament, but the idea frequently appears . . . . Nowhere in the New Testament is there a clearly defined doctrine of conscience, or even a description of it. The most illuminating passage in the New Testament on the nature of conscience is Romans 2:14, 15."[7]

> Conscience is an ideal Moses, and thunders from an invisible Sinai.
> —Hutton, in Augustus Strong, *Systematic Theology*

If law is not internalized in conscience, then conscience must be externalized in law. . . . Laws are not passed to make bad people good, but innocent people safe.
—Paul Tillich

Conscience is "the knife-edge that all our values press upon us whenever we are acting . . . contrary to these values.
—Gordon Allport, *The Individual and His Religion*

About morals I know only that that which is moral is what you feel good after, and what is immoral is what you feel bad after.
—Ernest Hemingway, in Will Durant, *Interpretations of Life*

If conscience only judges, what saves? Thus, we enter Romans 2:17-29 with that question.

Carnal Security (Romans 2:17-29)

(1) Law cannot save the Jew (2:17-24);
(2) circumcision cannot save the Jew (2:25-29).[8]

While no name tag is attached to his opponent in 2:1-16, in 2:17-29 Paul took to task his Jewish compatriots (see vss. 17, 28, and 29). Furthermore, his condemning generalization of 2:1 now becomes specified in 2:17-23. The buildup of verses 17-20 is followed by the bombshells of verses 21-23.

Note the recurring emergence of the word "law" (vss. 17, 18, 20, 23, 25, 26, 27). In verses 17-20 Paul demonstrated, probably somewhat sarcastically, that the average Jew is indeed a privileged character. Spiritually speaking, the Jew had his version of ivy-covered mansion, Rolls Royce, lakeside pool and gardens, etc.

The buildup in verses 17-20 is five pronged—with the last two prongs having multiple barbs on them:

(1) "if you rely on the law
(2) and brag about your relationship to God;
(3) if you know his will
(4) and approve of what is superior, being instructed by the law;
(5) if you are convinced that you are a guide for the blind, a light for those who are in the dark, an instructor of the foolish, a teacher of infants . . . ."

Rest (vs. 17, KJV) can be a beneficial blessing, but the opponent Paul had in mind was sound asleep in his lethargy toward the Law. Their snug relationship had become a smug relationship. C. H. Spurgeon said it was as if "a blind man [should be] elevated to the chair of optics in a university, a deaf man appointed to lead a symphony orchestra, a toad trying to teach eaglets to fly." This was a carnal security for these religious Rip van Winkles. However, while they had "just settled down for [their] long winter's nap," Paul was "out on the lawn" raising "such a clatter."

The Jew was both instructed ("know his will"; "instructed by the law") and insightful ("approve of what is superior" vs. 18). The last phrase may be translated: "He accepted as approved by testing the things that really matter."[9]

Verses 17 and 18 are God oriented, whereas verses 19-23 are others oriented. God's people were to act as Seeing Eye dogs to the blind, as lighthouses to the lost (vs. 19). Within their possession was the shaping mold of God's truth (vs. 20).

? Does your church in any way correspond to the privileged people of God described in Romans 2:17-20? If so, how?

After the big buildup of verses 17-20 came the monumental letdown of verses 21-23. Despite all the above accrued advantages (in vss. 17-20), "when they reach their crest, they break to pieces like a wave."[10] With five battering questions Paul reduced their tower of babble to rubble.

Ralph Martin paraphrased the beginning question: "Well, Mr. Teacher-of-Others, do you teach yourself?"[11] Paul knew of Jews who commanded others not to steal and not to worship idols, yet themselves stole from idol temples. Philo the Alexandrian Jew from Egypt, who lived during Christ's time, also coupled stealing, adultery, and temple-robbing together just as Paul did, showing us that Paul was not scraping up some isolated illustration. E. H. Gifford concluded, "The first clause [of vs. 23] is a summary of verses 17-20, the last a decisive answer to the four questions of verses 21, 22."[12] If a good teacher has been called an "animated question mark," then Paul was a top-notch teacher.[13] "Gotcha," he could say, if he wanted to taunt them.

? What kind of psychological process can shift us from being sincere to insincere?

It is all too easy for religious people to hibernate within ceremonialism. Hence, in Romans 2:25-29 Paul takes on the great bastion of many Jews' spiritual shelter—"circumcision." Circumcision had spiritual significance attached to it when instituted by God (Gen. 17:9-14; cf. the strange story of Ex. 4:24-26). However, just as the rich often use tax shelters to protect themselves against paying taxes, so circumcision had come to be a sign of automatic spiritual okayness (cp. Jn. 8:39-41) for numerous Jews.

Nevertheless, Paul the Jew raises the question of what constitutes authentic Jewishness. The point of 2:25-29 is: outward religious matters (e.g., circumcision) are only valid when what is inward really matters. Compare the assertions from Jewish writings below:

> **Jubilees 1:23**—"I will circumcise the foreskin of their heart and make a holy spirit for them."
>
> **Odes of Solomon 11:1, 2**—"My heart was circumcised . . . for the most High circumcised me by His Holy Spirit."
>
> **Deuteronomy 10:16**—"Circumcise your hearts."
>
> **Deuteronomy 30:6**—"The Lord your God will circumcise your hearts."
>
> **Romans 2:29**—"Circumcision is . . . of the heart, by the Spirit."

The Ann Landers Effect (Rom. 3:1-8)

The question of 2:25-29 is epitomized in 3:1—"what value is there in circumcision?" Or, more broadly, "What advantage, then, is there in being a Jew?" (3:1).

To tackle this issue, Paul plies the Ann Landers effect. That is, he conducts a question and answer session with his readers.

QUESTION	ANSWER
1. What advantage is there to Jewishness? (3:1)	1. The Jews were the bank vault of "the very words of God" (3:2)
2. Does my faithlessness cancel God's faithfulness? (3:3)	2. "Not at all!" Proof-texted by Psalm 51:4 (3:4)
3. If my unrighteousness showcases God's righteousness, why should He judge me? (3:5)	3. "God [will] judge the world" (3:6)
4. If my falseness showcases God's truthfulness, why should He judge me? (3:7)	4. Might as well say: "Let us do evil that good may result" (3:8)

The terms "condemned" (3:7) and "condemnation" (3:8) become the launching pad to the next section (3:20), showing that "the whole world" is under condemnation (3:19). Is there any route out of all this gloom and doom? Stay tuned.

CHAPTER
3

DISGRACE AND GRACE
Romans 3:10—4:8

> The epistle to the Romans is the true masterpiece of the New Testament and the very purest gospel, which is well . . . deserving that a Christian . . . should not only learn it by heart, word for word, but also that he should daily deal with it as the daily bread of men's souls. It can never be too much or too well read or studied. —Martin Luther

Concerning the section to be studied in this chapter, Donald G. Barnhouse said that "the epistle to the Romans has the most complete diagnosis of the plague of man's sin, and the most glorious setting forth of the simple remedy of justification by faith apart from the works of the law."[1]

The Divine Diagnosis (Rom. 3:9-20)

These twelve verses introduce us to Club Cosmic—the one club in which everyone in the world is a bona fide member. No elitism here. All hoity-toityness is ousted here, for we are dealing with the democratic doctrine of depravity.

25

"Total depravity does not mean that everyone is as thoroughly depraved in his actions as he could be, not that everyone will indulge in every form of sin, nor that a person cannot appreciate and even do acts of goodness; but it does mean that the corruption of sin extends to all [people] and to all parts of all [people] so that there is nothing within the natural [person] that can give him [saving] merit in God's sight."[2]

Paul agreed with II Chronicles 6:36—"there is no one who does not sin." The English word for "sin" is found over 45 times in Romans. In Romans 3:10-18 Paul welds together chain links from Scripture sources, virtually all from the Psalms, to forge his point—that all are "under sin" (3:9).

 Existentialists such as Kierkegaard, Jean-Paul Sartre, and Albert Camus have all exposed the moral nakedness of man.
—Eugene Nida, *Religion Across Cultures*

Three times (3:10-12) Paul, quoting Psalm 14:1-3, asserts "there is no one" who is sin exempt.

How do you reconcile Romans 3:11 ("no one . . . seeks") with Jeremiah 29:13; Acts 17:27 and Hebrews 11:6? How do you reconcile Romans 3:12 ("no one . . . good") with Luke 6:33; Acts 10:2; and Romans 2:7, 14?

In picturesque fashion, Paul paints humanity in 3:11, 12 as being like a lost caravan in a vast desert, a world gone A.W.O.L., a species having "become worthless" like souring milk. He diagnoses their:

"throats" (3:13);　　"lips" (3:13);　　　　　"feet" (3:15).
"tongues" (3:13);　　"mouths" (3:14); and

The pathology of our biology puts us under God's quarantine. In the great world courtroom all are declared guilty (3:19). The sinner stands unshielded, unspeaking, unmasked.

Knowledge of sin is the beginning of salvation.   —the Roman Seneca

By the law is the knowledge of sin.   —Paul (Rom. 3:20, KJV)

Paul's Prognosis—Doctrinal Diamonds (Rom. 3:21-26)

Romans 3:21 ("But now") is the Grand Canyon and Great Divide for the Book of Romans up to this point. Seminary president Alva McClain said, "I have always been sorry that when they divided the Bible into chapters, they did not begin one there [at 3:21]."[3]

Romans 1:1—3:20	the wrath of God is revealed	the malady of sin
Romans 3:21—8:39	the righteousness of God is revealed	the remedy of salvation

Alva McClain also said that if all the Bible were taken away and he could only keep six verses, he would have selected Romans 3:21-26.[4] Because of the dark velvet backdrop of Romans 1:18—3:20, these facets of the divine diamond glisten all the more brilliantly.

How can this righteousness from God be at the same time *apart from* the law, yet attested *by* the Law? Paul amplified the first phrase in verse 27 by maintaining that one "is justified by faith apart from observing the law." The second "Law" is capitalized in the NIV, showing that it refers to all of the Old Testament except the books of "the Prophets."

Charles Williams translated one of the picturesque terms for "sins" (in Col. 2:13) as "shortcomings." The idea fits nicely into the last part of Romans 3:23. We might imagine a home run hitter blasting a pitcher's fastball 420 feet to the center field wall. However, if the wall is 425 feet from home plate and a Willie Mays makes a one-handed grab of the ball at the top of the wall, the length of the blast makes no more difference in the score than if the batter had gone down swinging. His smash has "fall[en] short" of home run territory.

The person standing in the deepest valley or on top of Mt. Everest are both vastly "short" in terms of closeness to the distant moon.[5] Thus, there is a sense in which all humanity should have a true inferiority complex, for all are inferior in light of the shimmering perfection of God.

For the first time in Romans (3:24) the strategic word "justified" appears. "The noun . . . 'justification' is not used frequently in the Bible—only twice by Paul [though the verb is found fairly often] in his famous Epistle to the Romans, which may be regarded as the greatest single treatise in the Scriptures and in all literature on the subject."[6]

The subject of justification is central to Romans 3:19—5:21. To justify essentially means "to declare righteous" (as in a court of law). But Deuteronomy 25:1 (KJV) declares that a human judge "shall justify the righteous, and condemn the wicked." If "there is no one righteous" (Rom. 3:10), how can God, the Supreme Judge of the universe, justify the ungodly (Rom. 4:5)? Wouldn't that make God a crooked Judge? As one commentator paradoxically put it: "Grace is a form of divine injustice."[7] Yet, Paul affirms that God is "just and the justifier of the one who has faith in Jesus." (Rom. 3:26, NASB).

How then can God justly justify the unjust? The answer emerges in the stanza:

> God could not pass the sinner by;
> His sin demands that he must die;
> But in the cross of Christ we see
> How God can save us righteously.
> —Albert Midlane

On the basis of Christ's dying—"the just for the unjust" (I Pet. 3:18, KJV)—this riddle can be solved. God is both just and the justifier of the sinner who believes in Jesus, the Just One. Not only are we justified (i.e., pronounced righteous), but God is justified (i.e., vindicated) in what He did. Justification (for many scholars) involves two features:

(1) the canceling of our sin (or forgiveness, Rom. 4:7); and
(2) the crediting to us of Christ's righteousness (or imputation, Rom. 4:5; I Cor. 1:30; II Cor. 5:21).

BIOGRAPHICAL COMMENTARIES ON ROMANS 3:24 AND 25
John Bunyan said, "As I was walking up and down in the house, as a man in a most woeful state, that word of God took hold of my heart, you are 'justified freely by his grace through the redemption that is in Christ Jesus.' But oh, what a turn it made upon me! Now was I as one awakened out of some troublesome sleep and dream and . . . . It was as

if I had heard it thus expounded to me: Sinner, you think that because of your sins and infirmities I cannot save your soul, but behold my Son is by me, and upon Him I look and not on you, and will deal with you according as I am pleased with Him."

—older English altered from *Grace Abounding*

William Cowper (who wrote the hymn "God Moves in a Mysterious Way") said: "One day when I was walking the floor, I decided to pick up the Bible and see if there was anything to help me. My eye fell upon Romans 3:25. I saw the light in that verse and it saved me!"

—in Alva McClain, *Romans: The Gospel of God's Grace*

Redemption (3:24)—Christ's payment of the ransom price in buying the enslaved sinner from the marketplace of sin.

Propitiation (3:25, KJV)—Christ's satisfaction of the holy anger of God in His revulsion against sin.

Bragging Liquidated (Rom. 3:27-31)

I'm Okay, You're Okay was a fairly familiar book title of the 1970's, popularizing a brand of affirming psychology. Christian psychologist Newton Maloney said that the message of Romans is: "I'm not okay, you're not okay; but that's okay (because God has provided a way to make us okay)." This okayness is the issue at the heart of Romans and of the whole Bible. The theological term for being made "okay," or all right as far as God is concerned, is justification.

God is the Okayer. He is the One who has taken the initiative to set things straight, although we humans were the ones who took the initiative in messing things up (Gen. 3).

Many pro baseball teams have a relief pitcher whom they call "the stopper." With his fireball, a Goose Gossage or a Bruce Sutter is paid to come into a game in the late innings and "silence the guns" (i.e., bats) of the opposing team. In Romans 3:27 Paul becomes "the stopper." Or, rather, the Christian message becomes the silencer.

Can anyone afford a brag session in the presence of God? Romans 3:27 roundly answers that question: bragging "is completely shut out." Like some Mafia hit man liquidating a rival, all bragging is emphatically eliminated in the case of human salvation.

On what basis is bragging eliminated? The Law is not the liquidator. Bragging is eliminated "by the law [meaning 'the principle'] of faith" (3:27). An old hymn puts it:

> Boasting excluded, pride I abase;
> I'm only a sinner saved by grace.

29

J. B. Phillips captures the essence of verse 27 happily: "The whole matter is now on a different plane—believing instead of achieving." As John Murray put it, "Faith is self-renouncing; works are self-congratulatory."[8]

Martin Luther commented, "A Christian . . . is free from all things; he needs no works in order to be justified and saved, but receives these gifts in abundance from his faith alone."[9] A little poem capsules the relationship neatly:

> I cannot work my soul to save,
> For that my Lord has done;
> Yet I would work like any slave
> In love for God's dear Son.

Another way of emphasizing this truth is: A person is justified (or saved) by faith alone, but the faith that justifies is never alone.

WHEN ADDING SUBTRACTS
In "Rock of Ages" Augustus Toplady informed us:

> Not the labors of my hands
> Can fulfill Thy laws demands;
> Could my zeal no respite know,
> Could my tears forever flow,
> All for sin could not atone;
> Thou must save and Thou alone.
>
> Nothing in my hand I bring,
> Simply to Thy cross I cling . . . .

Galatians stresses that to add to Christ's work is to subtract from Christ's work for us (Gal. 2:16, 21). William Hendriksen stated it in a nutshell: to supplement the work of Christ by our work is to supplant it. See also Ephesians 2:8-10 and Titus 3:5, 8 for clarification of the relationship between faith and works.

If it is true that God employs this one method of salvaging humanity, then that must include Gentiles—as well as Jews—under its one umbrella (3:29). This one method of salvation cascades forth from the "one God" (3:30). The Jew who recited every Sabbath at the start of a synagogue service, "The Lord our God, the Lord is one" (Deut. 6:4), would have to have recognized that the "one God" is God of the Gentiles, too.

Although the Greek prepositions in verse 30 ("by" = *dia*, or "by means of," and "through" = *ek*, or "springing from") are different, some scholars hold that these are just literary variations. The important thing, as Lorman Petersen observed, is: "The Bible never says man [generically speaking] is justified on account of faith or because of faith but by or through faith."[10] In other words, faith is not a basis or cause of merit on our part before God; it is simply the God-given means by which we rely upon Him and receive His gifts.

This brand of thinking would have raised a red flag to the average Jewish mind, which Paul anticipated in 3:31. "Paul, if you say that all you have to do is to believe, doesn't that scratch completely any obligation to the Old Testament moral Law?" Although Paul went on to tackle such questions in a more amplified manner in Romans 6 and 7, here (in 3:31) he stamps his foot, "May it never be" (NASB).

God the Accountant (Rom. 4:1-5)

Americans are inordinate achievers. For example, the enterprising system called Amway symbolizes for some the American way. Americans grow up on gold stars, report cards, baseball hitting averages, medals, promotions, etc. Yet, in God's eyes all Christians are charity cases, coming for Heaven's handout. This is the divine welfare system of Paul—"to the [one] who does not work" (Rom. 4:5).

Romans 4:1-5 expounds the theme that we are not "justified by works" (4:2), but by faith (4:5). The word "faith" or "believe" is found 16 times in Romans four. The chapter may be outlined as follows:

Abraham's position—righteous by faith (4:1-12)
Abraham's possession—inheriting by faith (4:13-16)
Abraham's posterity—parenting by faith (4:17-25)

For Jewish people, Abraham was a kind of perennial Father's Day figure. In fact, his name is found in the New Testament more often than that of either Peter or Paul—about 64 times! Therefore, how do all the apostle's affirmations affect Abraham? Romans 4:2 is built on the underlying syllogism:

(1) Justified-by-works people can brag.
(2) Abraham might have claimed to be justified by works.
(3) Therefore, Abraham might have bragged.

However, in 3:27 Paul has already demolished any notion of bragging. No one can face God and brag (4:2). We might even paraphrase the "if" in verse two, "If that were the case, but it is not."

In order to buttress his doctrine of justification by faith (rather than works) Paul quoted Genesis 15:6. As Abraham stood out under the sky one starlit night, God informed him that his descendants would be as myriad as the stars. Abraham "believed [that is, had faith in] God; and it was credited to him as righteousness." Here are the 3 R's underlying Christianity:

(1) rely (or "believed");
(2) reckon (or "credited");
(3) righteousness.

In Gen. 15:6 we have the first appearance of the words believe, impute [or "count"], and righteousness. On "believed" H. C. Leupold wrote, "The biggest word in the chapter; one of the greatest in the Old Testament! Here is the first instance of the use of the word 'believe' in the Scriptures."[11]

Abraham's Accountant was God, and God credited righteousness to his account right then. The meaning is not that God accepted Abraham's faith instead of perfect righteousness as the meritorious ground for his justification.[12] Faith is not a substitute for righteousness. It does mean that Paul condemns good works as the basis of salvation. Works boast what we can do; faith receives what Christ has done and what Christ is.

In Romans 4 you will find the same Greek verb rendered "credited," (vs. 4, KJV 5, 9, 10, 11, 22, 23, 24). "The word translated 'reckon' (KJV) simply means 'think.' To reckon something is to think that it is so. Tamar was not a harlot, she was Judah's daughter-in-law. But he 'thought her to be an harlot; because she had covered her face' " (Gen. 38:15, KJV). In other words, righteousness "was set down on the credit side of the ledger."[13]

Justification by meritorious works and justification by God's grace are mutually exclusive of one another. There is nothing gracious about an employer who pays you a paycheck as the equivalent for hours worked (Rom. 4:4). A bonus may be an act of grace on the part of an employer, but not a salary paycheck.

In Romans 4 we are not merely in the office of Heaven's Welfare but in "the counting-room of the Great Accountant."[14] The individual in verse 5a is in contrast to the illustration in verse 4. Romans 4:5, in a nutshell, is Paul's doctrine of justification by faith. Commenting on Romans 4:5 the theologian James Denney wrote: "The whole Pauline gospel could be summed up in this one word—God who justifies the ungodly."[15]

The Council of Trent in 1545-1563 was the religious reaction to the discovery of the Reformers. In collision with the clear statement of Romans 4:5, the Canons and Decrees of the Council of Trent (chapter XVI, cannon IX) declared, "If anyone saith, that by faith alone the impious is justified in such wise to mean, that nothing else is required to cooperate in order to the obtaining of the grace of justification, and that it is not in any way necessary, let him be anathema."[16] It would seem that the Council of Trent pronounced the apostle Paul anathema! Paul maintained that a person "is justified by faith apart from observing the law" (Rom. 3:28; cp. 4:5).

> I am an empty vessel, not one thought
> Or look of love I ever to Thee brought,
> Yet I may come, and come again to Thee
> With this the empty sinner's only plea,
> "Thou lovest me."

'Done' Does in 'Do'

The old commercial advertized that "Duz Does Everything." "Does" or "Do" in the Christian framework only applies after one realizes that "Done" is the launching pad for Christianity—what Christ has done on the cross for my salvation. Salvation, translates the Living Bible in Romans 4:5, "is *given* to those who do *not* work for it."

An old hymn captures the essence:

> Done is the work that saves
> Once and for ever done;
> Finished the righteousness
> That clothes the unrighteous one.
> —Horatius Bonar

This was the truth discovered by John Wesley. Wesley had been reared in a Christian home. He studied for the ministry. He taught the New Testament in Greek. He visited prisoners in jail. He led the Holy Club at Oxford. He even went to America as a missionary to the Indians. Yet, en route back to England from America Wesley wrote, "I went to America to convert the Indians, but oh, who shall convert me?" It was only afterward at a Moravian meeting in Aldersgate Street that he wrote, "I felt I did trust in Christ alone for my salvation."

A minister wrote in to Billy Graham, saying that during one of Graham's crusades he realized that he had never himself actually been converted. In his newspaper column Billy Graham replied with the case of another prominent minister who related the same thing. Yes, only when a car has an engine will it run!

Sometimes people grow up in a Christian church with a kind of "osmosis" brand of religion. They have vague notions of the Christian faith—that "you do the best you can," "keep the golden rule," "live right," etc. They think that doing good is the essence of Christianity.

But F. F. Bruce captured the wonderfulness of Paul's pronouncement:

"God in the Gospel does the very thing which in the law He says He will not do (cf. Ex. 23:7: 'I will not acquit the wicked,' where LXX has the same verb and noun as Paul uses)."[17] God pronounces the ungodly okay because of the transfer of righteousness from God the Son—when it is received by faith!

Pardon in Pictures (Rom. 4:6-8)

In order to document "the happy state of the man whom God accounts righteous" (Rom. 4:6, J. B. Phillips) and to reinforce and illustrate the truth about Abraham, Paul quoted Psalm 32:1 and 2. David had been both an adulterer and an accomplice to assassination—not a particularly good record! David had broken three of God's cardinal commands (Ex. 20:13, 14, 17), yet he found forgiveness.

Salvation almost seems to be refracted through a pictorial prism in these verses, like the varied colors of a rainbow. Three pictorial forms present David's deliverance. First, sins are subtracted. Forgiveness is God's marvelous subtraction system. All of the minuses registered against us are removed. Secondly, our "sins are covered" (4:7). The Greek word behind "covered" is only found here in the New Testament. Thirdly, as previously indicated, God the Bookkeeper has intervened in our debt-heaped account to transfer His righteousness in place of our unrighteousness. All the incalculable charges that could be billed to us have been assumed by Christ, the Righteous One. No wonder the Gospel is Good News!

Here is the world's greatest transfer, history's greatest exchange. Donald Grey Barhouse put it, "I deserved hell. Jesus took my hell. Now Jesus offers me His heaven."

Count Nicolas von Zinzendorf (1700-60), Moravian leader, penned:

> Jesus, thy blood and righteousness
> My beauty are, my glorious dress.
> Midst flaming worlds in these arrayed,
> With joy shall I lift up my head.

Hymn writer Edward Mote added that the one who possesses Christ's imputed righteousness is

> Dressed in His righteousness alone,
> Faultless to stand before the throne.

It is as if Christ had taken our debt and handed His credit card of righteousness to us. This is the majestic doctrine of imputation.

CHAPTER
4
RIGHT WITHOUT RITES
Romans 4:9—5:21

Rites Won't Make You Right! (Rom. 4:9-25)

Two topics were taken up in Romans 2:17-29—
    (1) "the law" (five times in 2:17-24); and
    (2) "circumcision" (nine times as a noun or verb in 2:25-29).
In Romans 4:9-17 Paul returns to these same two topics (in reverse order) in Abraham's case:
    (1) circumcision (in 4:9-12);
    (2) the law (in 4:13-17).
Abraham was not put right with God through religious rites. Instead of by formalism, Abraham was justified by faith (which appears four times as a noun or verb in 4:18-25). In the final parallelism of Romans 4:25, Christ:

<blockquote>
"was delivered . . . to death
for [i.e., because of] our sins
and
was raised to life
for [i.e., because of] our justification."
</blockquote>

Probably the parallelism intends us to understand that as our sin triggered Christ's death, so our justification (completed in Christ's death) triggered His resurrection. The "justification" of Romans 4:25 becomes the takeoff point for being "justified" in 5:1.

The Beneficiary's Assets (Rom. 5:1-5)

Romans 1:17 (KJV) declared, "The just [or justified] shall live by faith." But what does it mean to "live"? Really living means:[1]
   (1) to be free from God's wrath (chap. 5),
   (2) to be free from sin (chap. 6),
   (3) to be free from the law (chap. 17), and
   (4) to be free from death (chap. 8).

Justification (being put right with God) is like a mighty river channel, and Romans 5 maps out the tributaries that proceed from the water source. Believers are beneficiaries of a policy with spiritual wealth. "Since we have been given right standing with God through faith," reads the Charles B. Williams Version of Romans 5:1, "let us continue enjoying . . . " the dividends that are ours.

Ω There is some question about whether the Greek word for "have" means "we have" (objective fact) or "let us have" (subjective invitation), depending on whether the Greek "o" is long or not. First, it could mean that at Calvary God has declared an armistice for Christians. Like the turning weather vane, no matter which way the wind blows, we still have our standing of peace with God.

A second way to understand the verb is "let us enjoy the possession of peace"[2] or "let us grasp the fact that we have peace" (J. B. Phillips).

Isaiah 32:17 (KJV) says poetically:

> And the work [result] of righteousness
>   shall be peace;
> and the effect of righteousness
>   [shall be] quietness and assurance . . . .

God has spread out the "welcome mat" for us, so we can relax.

A second dividend of justification is that "we have access" (5:2) to God. "In the ancient world a king was heavily guarded, not only by his retinue of soldiers, but also by the red tape of officialdom."[3] Unlike a president who is guarded by Secret Service agents or an executive whose path is blocked by numerous receptionists in waiting rooms, God is ACCESSIBLE. There are no "Keep Out" signs cluttering His door. The word "access" refers to getting close to something, such as when "engines of war are brought close to the walls of a besieged city."[4] God is Someone you can get close to.

Ω One interesting secular Greek usage of the Greek word for "access" is found in the historian Xenophon.[5] He tells how war prisoners were "brought into the presence" of the Persian king Cyrus. It was the job of the king's cup-bearer to "introduce" to the king appropriate visitors. He held the job of introducer much akin to a modern receptionist in a doctor's office. Jesus is the Christian's Introducer, the Go-between who grants us admittance to the presence of God. What a wealth in the word "access"!

Another secular Greek use of "access" is found in the Greek writer Plutarch. He uses it for "a place for ships to put in."[6] Plutarch refers to a general drawing up his troops before a harbor where there was no *prosagoge* [the Greek word for "access" in Rom. 5:2]. Thus, Barclay commented, "Jesus opened to us a way into the haven of God's grace. We are like storm-tossed mariners who would make shipwreck of life unless Jesus took over the piloting of the ship of life and steered it out of the storm into the safe haven of the grace of God."[7]

With such dividends we can "rejoice in the hope of the glory of God" (5:3). We don't need to be "glumbums," as Ray Stedman put it.[8] Stedman further remarked that some Christians already look like they "have been marinated in embalming fluid."[9]

K. E. Kirk called the style of Romans 5:3-5 "a 'sorites' or chain-catalogue, of a type popular with the Stoics of St. Paul's day."[10] In verses 3-5 we find a

(1) pressurized environment ("suffering");
(2) persevering endurance ("perseverance");
(3) proven experience ("character");
(4) prospective expectation ("hope"); and
(5) poured out experience ("God has poured out his love into our hearts").

The reason a believer has the capacity to rejoice in sufferings is the circle of interlocking benefits diagrammed below (clockwise).

6.
(therefore, we have come full circle back to hope) (vs. 5)

1.
"rejoice in . . . hope"
(vs. 2)

2.
"rejoice in our sufferings"
(vs. 3)

5.
character produces "hope"
(vs. 4)

4.
"endurance [produces] tested character"
(vs. 4, Williams)

3.
"suffering produces endurance"
(vs. 3, Williams)

To do the will of God requires a certain amount of tension. Muscle growth demands friction; plant growth demands rain; Christian growth calls for "sufferings" (5:3). This is hard for many of us to admit. "Many Christians have an ejection seat mentality . . . . [They want to] pull the ejection cord and zip off into glory."[11]

TRIALS CAN BE TRANSMUTED INTO TRIUMPHS
"Lewis Carroll suffered migraine headaches, which inspired parts of *Alice's Adventures in Wonderland*. For instance, there are a few episodes in the story when people change sizes and when a blind spot appears to someone trying to focus his vision. Size distortion and blank spotting are two classic symptoms of migraine headache." Apparently Carroll let his problems work for him.[12]

One thorn of experience is worth a whole wilderness of warning.
—James Russell Lowell

Experience is a good school, but the fees are high.   —Heinrich Heine

The word "character" could be properly used of silver that has been refined in the fire, thereby taking the shape of approved character. No wonder this is possible; we have total Trinity at work for us and in us ("The Holy Spirit," vs. 5; "God" and "Christ," vs. 8).

The last tributary in Romans 5:1-5, flowing from the mainstream of justification, is that "God has poured out his love into our hearts by the Holy Spirit" (5:5, NIV).

F. B. Meyer described God's love as "the Amazon River flowing down to water one daisy."
—in Ian Macpherson, *The Art of Illustrating Sermons*

TURN ON THE TAP
A vast metropolis like Chicago must have a mammoth water supply. Lake Michigan provides such a source and repository. But how shall the average human take advantage of Lake Michigan's provisions? Means are provided—a network of pipelines. Still that water only does a person any good when the basic condition is met—he or she must turn on the faucet.

God has an inexhaustible supply of love to pour out (Rom. 5:5), but unless we seek Him in faith, none of those benefits will rightly become ours.[13]

Arthur S. Way paraphrased verse 5: "the brimming river of God's love has already overflowed into our hearts, on-drawn by His Holy Spirit, which He has given to us." Like the two sons of the widow that Elisha helped, we bring our "empty vessels" (II Ki. 4:1-7) to be filled by a seemingly endless source. Then, as Cynthia Clawson sings, we need to " . . . carry the water to the desert; Gotta stop this haulin' water to the sea."

Love's Rarity and Audacity (Romans 5:6-8)

God's acting for us in Christ is like receiving a rare, alien, and imported plant as a gift. Verses 6-8 make this clear. Ordinary humans don't ordinarily act toward each other the way God has acted toward us. There are three look-alike words in Greek in verses 6-8 used to describe our condition:

(1) *asthenon* = "powerless," vs. 6;
(2) *asebon* = "ungodly," vs. 6; and
(3) *[h]amartolon* = "sinners" vs. 8.

Ω The term "rarely" in Romans 5:7 can be illuminated by comparing Acts 27:16, which could be rendered, "we were scarcely [the same Greek word as in Rom. 5:7] able to get the boat under control." Placing ourselves in the mindset of embattled sailors who are "scarcely" able to cope with a furious seastorm, we can sense the difficulty in the word.

A sampling of translations of verse 8 below helps us appreciate the verb.

"God proves His own love" (Berkeley Version).
"God shows his love" (RSV).
"God demonstrates his own love" (NIV).
"God renders conspicuous" (Charles Hodge).
"God presses home" (Sanday and Headlam).

Ω The titanic truth of Scripture is that "while we were still sinners, Christ died for us" (vs. 8). The Greek word for "for" is *huper*. If a person in the Greek-speaking world was illiterate, in place of his name he would sign *huper* (we would say, mark "X"). Similarly, Christ died on our behalf, in our place, as our stand-in.

Beyond Armistice (Rom. 5:9-11)

C. S. Lewis, British author and champion of Christianity, once said, "We are not merely imperfect creatures who must be improved; we are . . . rebels who must lay down our arms."[14] In the Old Testament God is occasionally depicted as a Warrior (see Hab. 3:9, 11, 12). In general (due to sin) the Bible depicts ours as a planet in rebellion. We are "enemies" to God (Col. 1:21).

Despite humanity's ungodly hostility and unholy war against God,

God Himself provided the magnanimous, sacrificial, magnificent basis for armistice. His peace treaty, as it were, has been signed in the inkwell of Calvary.

> God in the gospel of His Son
> > Makes His eternal council known.
> We read in characters of blood
> > The wisdom, power, and grace of God.

George Ladd said, "We have peace with God in that God is now at peace with us."[15]

Paul used an argument from the lesser ("if") to the greater ("much more") in Romans 5:9-11. Obviously, he used the ordinarily synonymous terms "justified" and "saved" in verse 9 in a different sense—one past and the other future. This can be seen in the comparison charted between verses 9 and 10.

ALREADY	NOT YET
"now . . . justified" (vs. 9)	"shall . . . be saved" (vs. 9)
"we were reconciled"	"shall . . . be saved" (vs. 10)

The drift of these verses was summarized by Charles Hodge: "If Christ has died for his enemies, He will surely save his friends."[16] Since "the wrath of God is being revealed from heaven against all . . . godlessness" (1:18) and we are "the ungodly" (5:6), it follows that we need to be "saved from God's wrath" (5:9).

✖ Paul's principal theological terms are pictorial. Reconciliation [5:10, 11] depicts people as rebel-warriors against God; justification views them as law-breakers arraigned before God, the Supreme Court Judge.[17] We are guilty; therefore, we need to be justified. We are at odds, therefore, we need to be reconciled. Reconciliation is also the subject in Ephesians 2:13-22 and Colossians 1:20-22 in addition to Romans 5 and II Corinthians 5.

Charles Wesley penned:

> My God is reconciled;
> > His pardoning voice I hear . . . ."

Despite Wesley's hymn line, the New Testament itself never explicitly says "God is reconciled." Rather, the New Testament speaks of the "world" or "us" as *objects* of God's work of reconciliation. II Corinthians 5 speaks of reconciliation in two ways, as charted below.

transacting past and objective (vs. 19)	"God . . . reconciled us" (vs. 18) "God was reconciling the world"
invitation present and subjective	"Be reconciled" (vs. 20)

In the Greek of that time the word for "reconciliation" had an interesting background. "Katallasein in ordinary secular Greek acquires the almost technical sense of changing money, or changing into money. Plutarch tells how four Syrian brothers stole the king's gold vessels in Corinth and how bit by bit they changed them into money."[18] Because of the Great Exchange (Christ's righteousness for our sin) God can change us into people who please Him.

Despite the ravages of World War II, a Norwegian major said to the press as he looked away to snowclad peaks beyond the rubble of bombed buildings, "The mountains are still ours." Romans 5:1-11 is the adult equivalent of "visions of sugarplums" dancing through our heads. Said the hymn writer:

> More wonderful it seems
> Than all the golden fancies
> Of all our golden dreams.

Donald Grey Barnhouse of Philadelphia preached a sermon on all the treasured truths that belong to Christians because of Christ. From the first row of the balcony a boy's eyes were riveted on the preacher. After the service the boy greeted Barnhouse at the door with the words, "Boy, Doc, we sure are sittin' pretty, aren't we?"

Yes, look at the dividends of Romans 5:1-11. We have a:
legacy of peace (vs. 1);
right of access (vs. 2);
bequest of joy (vss. 2, 3, 11);
heirloom of endurance (vs. 3);
chest of character (vs. 4);
grant of love (vs. 5); and
claim of salvation (vss. 9, 10).

"What a wonderful Savior!"

The Two Fountainheads (Rom. 5:12-21)

"Verses 12-21 . . . are perhaps the most peculiar in all the epistle. Paul's thoughts leap forth like a torrential mountain stream. They rush with such force that they do not always come to carefully formed expression."[19] Observe the progress of thought below.

Condemnation (Rom. 1:1—3:20)
Justification (Rom. 3:21—5:11)
Relationship between Condemnation and Justification (Rom. 5:12-21)

> What may be called the starting point of Christian theology, the doctrine of hereditary guilt and sin, through the fall of Adam, and of the consequent entire and helpless corruption of our nature, is entirely unknown to Rabbinical Judaism.
> —Alfred Edersheim, *The Life and Times of Jesus the Messiah, I*

The basic structure of Romans 5:12-21 is:

(1) an incomplete thesis (5:12);
(2) an interrupting parenthesis (5:13-17);
(3) an involved synthesis (5:18-21).

Like Schubert's Unfinished Symphony or Charles Dickens's *The Mystery of Edwin Drood*, Romans 5:12 launches its thesis before becoming absorbed in an intricate yarn of entangled mystery. John Murray assumes that Paul's finished sentence would have read:

As through one man sin entered into the world and death through sin, and so death passed upon all (for all sinned), even so through one man righteousness entered into the world and life through righteousness, and so life passed to all (for all were accounted righteous).

> No man is an island, entire of itself; every man is a piece of the continent, a part of the main. If a clod is washed away, Europe is the less as well as if a promontory were or a manor of thy friends. Every man's death diminishes me, because I am involved in mankind. And therefore never send to know for whom the bell tolls: it tolls for thee.
> —John Donne

> In Adam's fall
> We sin-ned all. —"A" in *The New England Primer*

> We are implicated in the story of Adam.
> —Ernst Kasemann, *Commentary on Romans*

The quintessential truth of Romans 5:12 is that when Adam sinned, all sinned. As Ralph Martin put it, "All are declared to have actually and actively sinned with Adam."[20] A national leader acts for the people of his country, and the his decision will involve all in either as wise choice or an error.

Sin was Death's John the Baptist. As John the Baptist heralded the entrance of the Christ, so sin heralded the entrance of death. "We Three Kings of Orient Are" had nowhere near as great an influence on humanity as the four kings of Romans 5:12-21. They are (from the Berkeley Version):

(1) "sin reigned" (vs. 21);
(2) "death is king" (vs. 17);
(3) "grace reign[s]" (vs. 21); and
(4) Christians "reign as kings" (vs. 17).

While the word "type" (as in "typology") never appears in the King James Version, Adam is the only Old Testament individual to be called (in Greek) a type of Christ (Rom. 5:14). "In God's sight," wrote Thomas Goodmin of Oxford (1600-1680), "there are two men—Adam and Jesus Christ—and these two men have all other men hanging at their girdle strings" (in F. F. Bruce, *The Epistle of Paul to the Romans*, p. 127). Thus, Paul lined up comparisons and contrasts of "the first man Adam" and "the last Adam" (I Cor. 15:45)—the two fountainheads.

The "just as" of Romans 5:18 resumes the thread of the "just as" initiated at 5:12. Reverberations of Isaiah 53 echo out in the last part of Romans 5.

ISAIAH 53	ROMANS 5
"justify" (vs. 11)	"justification" (vss. 16, 18)
"many" (vss. 11, 12)	"many" (vss. 15, 19)
"unto death" (vs. 12)	"death" (vss. 17, 21)
"bore the sin of many" (vs.12)	"many were made sinners" (vs. 19)

Early in church history Irenaeus (c. A.D. 175) observed the analogy that "by his obedience on a tree [cf. I Pet. 2:24; the Lord] renewed what was done [in Eden] by disobedience [with reference to] a tree."[21]

Romans 5 closes basically as do chapters 6 and 7—"through Jesus Christ our Lord."

5

WANTED: DEAD AND ALIVE

Romans 6

After what he felt was a particularly boring Sunday church service, a little boy sauntered through the church foyer while waiting for his parents. He became intrigued with the gold plaque hanging on the wall with its engraved list of names. When his parents finally arrived, the boy sidled up to the pastor in the greeting line to pose his question. He asked, "What are all those people's names on the wall over there?" The minister took on a somber look and replied, "Those are the names of all our people who died in the service." Reflecting on his recent experience, the little boy asked again, "Which one—the morning or the evening service?"

It's true that some church people are "dead" in the wrong way (see Rev. 3:1). Nevertheless, it's also true that there is a sense in which live people are to be dead and to *act* dead.

To Sin or Not to Sin? (Rom. 6:1-4)

✘ "It is in Romans 6—8 that we have the most extended teaching in the Bible on the ground and experimental outworking of sanctification."[1] Sanctification (or we might even say, saint-ification) or holiness is what happens to a saint (the noun from the same root word) or holy one (the corresponding adjective). Yet Biblical saints are not some unattainable elite corps of untainted individuals. In fact, Paul referred to some pretty scandalous sinners as "saints" (see I Cor. 1:2; cf. 3:1; 5:1, 2). Adam Clarke said, "Sanctification is the Christianizing of the Christian."[2]

Who is at work in this sanctifying process? "We are [being] changed . . . by the Spirit of the Lord" (II Cor. 3:18). Yet, "Our working is not dispensed with . . . because God works; God's working is not suspended because we work. There is the correlation and conjunction of both."[3]

Theologian Anders Nygren outlined Romans 6—8 as follows:

Chapter 6: we are free from sin—yet we must battle against it.
Chapter 7: we are free from the law—yet we are not righteous according to its criterion.
Chapter 8: we are free from death—yet we long for the redemption of our bodies[4]

Alva McClain capsuled Romans 6 and 7 this way: "Chapter 6 contains the right way of sanctification; and chapter 7, the wrong way."[5]

Ralph Martin[6] divided chapter 6 into:
(1) the charge of licence (6:1-14); and
(2) the charge of lawlessness (6:15-23).

In Romans 5:20 (using J. B. Phillips's rendition) "sin is shown to be wide and deep, [and] thank God his grace is wider and deeper still!" "But if that's so," some heckler of Paul might yell out from the crowd, "then we ought to sin it up to the hilt, so that grace can really have a heyday." A modern individual might follow this false reasoning this way: "This is the best of all possible worlds, for God loves to forgive sinners and I love to sin."[7] This incorrect logic has to be squelched. For a Christian, to sin or not to sin is not the question.

Correct Premise, Incorrect Conclusion

"A notable historical instance [of Romans 6:1] may be seen in the Russian monk Rasputin, the evil genius of the Romanov family in its last years of power . . . . He held that, as those who sin most require most forgiveness, a sinner who continues to sin with abandon enjoys, each time he repents, more of God's forgiving grace than any ordinary sinner."[8]

Believers are not to be wallowing in sin. As F. F. Bruce paraphrased verse 2, "There can be no peaceful coexistence between death to sin and life in sin."[9] Oil and water don't blend, and Christianity is an inveterate enemy of sin (6:2). John Murray stated, "The fact of having died to sin is the fundamental premise [or starting point] of the apostle's thought."[10] Like wrestlers whom the referee has signaled on the arms, we must make a clean break with sin.

To dramatize this death to sin, Paul brings up baptism. Romans 6:3-

5 is a classic set of verses on baptism, with verses 3 and 4 having the only mention of baptism in the entire book. Paul spoke of being "baptized into Jesus Christ" and "baptized into his death" (6:3). Observe the following parallel expressions:

"baptize them into the name" (Mt. 28:15, Williams Version);
"baptized into the name of Paul" (I Cor. 1:13);
"baptized into Moses" (I Cor. 10:2).

The expression "baptized into" carries overtones of being "identified with" or "associated with." To be "baptized into Christ Jesus" is to be "baptized into his death" (vs. 3). (Notice that "death" or "dead" is mentioned four times in verses 1-4, and fifteen times in some form in the first fourteen verses, thereby keying us into Paul's primary point.)

The lockstep sequence of ideas in the Gospel that "Christ died . . . and . . . he was buried [and] . . . was raised" (I Cor. 15:3, 4) becomes the takeoff point for the apostle's argument. Like Christ, so Christians. If Christ came back to life, even so Christians also . . . may live a new life (Rom. 6:4). Therefore, instead of being "dead in" sins (Eph. 2:1) we have "died to sin" (Rom. 6:2).

Wanted: Dead and Alive (Rom. 6:5-10)

Paul says Christians have been "planted together in the likeness" of Christ's death (6:5, KJV). The term "planted together" (that occurs only here in the New Testament) is "used of the man and the horse as grown together in the centaur by [the secular Greek writer] Lucian."[11] Just as the mythical half man, half horse are joined as one, so also is the believer united with Christ's death. Observe the parallelism:

"If we have been united with him . . . " (vs. 5),
"For we know (vs. 6);
"If we died with Christ" (vs. 8),
"For we know" (vs. 9).

"Our old self was crucified" with Christ (vs. 6). The "old self" has been defined as "the whole personality organized for, and geared in, rebellion against God."[12]

Why are Christians "crucified with" Christ (vs. 6)? We are co-crucified with Christ so "that the power of the sin-controlled body might be done away with" (Berkeley Version). We do not need to be sin's slaves.

Kenneth Wuest likened the Christian's situation to a record or tape that has been disengaged. (The word "destroyed" in Rom. 6:6 [A.V.] is translated "neutralized" by Weymouth, "rendered powerless" by The Twentieth Century New Testament, and "made ineffective and inactive for evil" by The Amplified Version. That old tape or script need not be constantly replayed, yet Christians still possess the power, as it were, to re-engage the record needle (Jas. 3:10; I Jn. 2:1).

Ω The Greek verb for "destroyed" is *katargeo* (*kaht-are-GEH-oh*). A simplified root-form of it is found in Matthew 20:3 ("doing nothing") in the parable about day-laborers. In the parable a hirer hired unemployed workers at four different staggered times. We could render the noun *argous* in Matthew 20:3 "out of a job." The prefix *kat-* on the front of our verb in Romans 6:6 simply intensifies the basic verb's meaning ("completely," "thoroughly"). In other words, we might say the verb means "to put completely out of a job." When we transport this insight over into Romans 6:6, we learn that the purpose of the believer's death with Christ is that the body as controlled by sin might be completely put out of a job. In other words, Christians should want to put sin in the unemployment line!

Sin is a slave driver, but "we should no longer be slave to" it (Rom. 6:6). In one sense we are "Wanted: Dead." The Berkeley Version supplies the reason: "A corpse is considered guiltless of sin" (6:7). Actually, the expression "freed from sin" (6:7) means "justified from sin." In other words, it is as if a judge has dismissed the case sin has against us. If we stand acquitted, then sin has no legal claim upon us.

If it has stopped raining outside, a child out of doors does not have to get wet. There is nothing in the air that demands the child's wetness. However, there are those tempting mud puddles left in the rain's aftermath. The child is rain-free, or is he? Christians are pronounced "dead to sin" (Rom. 6:2, KJV), that is, sin-free. However, that actuality must be part of our attitude ("count yourselves [mentally] dead to sin," 6:11) and actions ("put to death . . . whatever [sin] belongs to your earthly nature," Col. 3:5).

❝❝ Jesus Christ is brought in as a constitutional sovereign, but we retain the right to veto His leading, assuming the power of prime minister in the decisions made.   —Elliott Cole, in *Beside the Still Waters*

It has been said that if Galatians is the "Magna Charta" of the Gospel, Romans is the "Constitution."

—J. O. Buswell, *The Zondervan Pictorial Bible Dictionary*

Hence, Romans 6:7 provides the Christian's declaration of independence, the basis of our freedom.

Not only are Christians "Wanted: Dead" (vss. 6-8), but they are "Wanted: Dead *and* Alive" (vss. 10, 11). We are to live for God (vs. 10). Notice also the parallelism in verses 10 and 11.

vs. 10	Christ "died to sin once"	Christ "lives to God"
vs. 11	"yourselves dead to sin"	you "alive to God"

The Christian's Arsenal (Rom. 6:11-14)

In verses 1-10 Paul informed us of what *has happened* to us (we "were baptized," vs. 3; we "were . . . buried," vs. 4; "we have been united" with Christ, vs. 5; we were "crucified with him," vs. 6; we "died with Christ," vs. 8). In verses 11-14 Paul shifted to what *must happen* in us. We must:

(1) "count" ourselves "dead" (vs. 11);
(2) "not let sin reign" (vs. 12); and
(3) "offer" outselves (vs. 13).

Two characters were debating whether an animal they found was dead. One argued that it was, but the other kept seeing movement, revealing life. When the second finally witnessed the animal kick, he said, "It's like this. He's dead, but he just doesn't know it yet."

The paradoxical teaching of Romans 6:1-14 may be capsuled:

"if we died with Christ" (vs. 8), we must
"count [ourselves] dead to sin" (vs. 11).

In a long-ago village one shopkeeper hung out a sign: "We dye to live and live to dye; the more we live, the more we dye; and the more we dye, the more we live." Substituting "die" for "dye" provides us with an element of Paul's broader teaching. In Colossians 3:5 Paul commands us to "put to death" a series of sins. Here in Romans 6 he argues that we *are* actually dead (vss. 7, 8), but we must *act as if* we are dead (vs. 11).

'RECALLED TO LIFE'
One of Charles Dickens' better known books is *A Tale of Two Cities*. It is a tale alternating between London and Paris. It is set during the days of

the bloody revolution of the guillotine. In the story Dr. Manette is liberated after two years of imprisonment. In Dickens' historical novel are the unforgettable words, referring to Dr. Manette's release, "Recalled to Life." Likewise, the Christian is recalled to new, liberating life in Christ.

Romans 6:12-23 may be outlined as follows:

(1) Sin is an old monarch now defeated (12-14);
(2) Sin is an old master now deposed (15-23).[13]

The first point swivels upon the word "reign" (vs. 12). Christian David, a Moravian believer, spoke to John Wesley of sin remaining in him, but not reigning in him. Like King Herod—or many other potentates of Scripture—sin is a tyrant. However, for the Christian sin has been defrocked, dethroned. Sin only carries a papier mache scepter.

Charles Wesley poignantly penned the plight of the disobedient:

> Yet, O! ten thousand lusts remain,
>   And vex my soul absolved from sin;
> Still rebel nature strives to reign,
>   Still I am all unclean, unclean!
> —in Ernest Rattenbury, *The Evangelical Doctrines*
>   *of Charles Wesley's Hymns*

The Christian soldier (see Eph. 6:11-18) has an arsenal. J. B. Phillips renders Romans 6:13—"But, like men rescued from certain death, put yourselves in God's hands as weapons of good for his own purposes."

Ω The Greek word for "instruments" (vs. 13) is used elsewhere for ship's tackle, tools, and weapons.[14] The weapons we fight with are not weapons of the world. On the contrary, they have divine power to demolish strongholds (II Cor. 10:4).

❝❝ The Christian life is the only battle where victory depends upon complete surrender.   —Source unknown

Sigmund Freud[15] likened the still-unchanged areas of people's lives to nature parks that the city fathers had fenced off within metropolitan areas, so that citizens could have a little piece of the old life to wander in and recall the way it used to be.

What do we do as Christians if we discover that we still have these unaltered areas that remain untamed in our Christian experience? We must yield ourselves (6:12, 13) to God so as to be wielded by Him as His instruments.

The German composer Mendelssohn visited the cathedral at Fridbourg. He desired an opportunity to play the magnificent organ there. He was unannounced by name to the old organist at the cathedral who did not want this stranger touching his organ at first. Finally the protective keeper of the organ yielded. After listening in amazement to the sounds emerging from his organ, he asked the stranger, "Who are you?" When he heard the name, he exclaimed, "Can it be that I so nearly let Mendelssohn not touch this organ!" The instrument yielded to the master made a world of difference.

King Arthur carried a jeweled sword named Excaliber. Sir Launfal was commanded to take the sword and hurl it into the lake. Launfal disobeyed and hid it several times, but finally discharged his duty. The story says that a giant mystical hand emerged from the lake, brandished the sword several times, and drew it under water. The point of the story: he was not throwing the instrument away, but only returning it to the rightful owner.

Ray Stedman makes the whole matter quite down to earth. He observed that we sit down to a meal with our God-given appetite. However, there always enters the temptation of eating more than we should. If we allow our body to be controlled by sin at that point, we become gluttons and gourmands. "A gourmand," Stedman explains, "is someone who . . . lives for the taste of [luxurious] food."[16] Consequently, even in eating—which we all must do—we can be either controlled by physical appetites or yielded to God.

> He breaks the power of cancelled sin;
> He sets the prisoner free.
> His blood can make the foulest clean;
> His blood availed for me.

Whose Am I? (Rom. 6:15-23)

"A new servitude—there is something to that," soliloquized Jane Eyre as she tried to extricate herself from her miserable school-teaching situation.

Christians ought to be "as free . . . as servants," said Peter paradoxically (I Pet. 2:16). Paul's paradox pictures the Christian as formerly "slaves to sin . . . [but] free from . . . righteousness" (6:20) and now "free from sin and . . . slaves to God" (6:22). The term "slaves" is found seven times in Romans 6:15-23.

50

These offsetting opposites are part of numerous pairings.

NORTH POLE	SOUTH POLE
grace (vs. 15)	law (vs. 15)
righteousness (vs. 19)	impurity (vs. 19)
righteousness (vs. 20)	sin (vs. 20)
eternal life (vs. 22)	death (vs. 21)
gift (vs. 23)	wages (vs. 23)

"You are under obligation to [your benefactor] Mrs. Reid," Jane Eyre, the orphaned child, was told. So, sinners are under obligation to Sin the Tyrant.

When one is living under a dictator of a country, he has no choice but to obey the laws of that dictatorship. If the dictator is overthrown by a democratic regime and sent into exile into another country, the citizens are free to live a new kind of life.
—Charles Ryrie, *Balancing the Christian Life*

Paul enunciates a freedom greater than any of Franklin D. Roosevelt's Four Freedoms (freedom of speech, freedom from fear, freedom from want, and freedom of religion). Paul's fifth freedom is to be "set free from sin" (6:22).

> My will is not mine own
>   Till Thou hast made it thine;
> If it would reach a monarch's throne,
>   It must its crown resign.
> Make me a captive, Lord,
>   And then I shall be free;
> Force me to render up my sword,
>   And I shall conqueror be.
> —George Matheson

If you are not ready to surrender everything to God, are you ready to say, "I am willing to be made willing"?
—F. B. Meyer, in Ralph Earle, *The Quest of the Spirit*

A child watched in amazement as a roof repairman walked freely atop his family's barn roof. The climber had no cleats, yet he walked upright and freely around the rooftop. The child's natural curiosity sought the solution to this amazing feat. The solution was found, upon closer inspection, to be that another man was on the ground on the opposite of the barn. The second man held tightly to a rope which was wrapped around the repairman. Whenever the roof repairman wanted more rope, he would call for it, and his ground-level companion would release the rope inch by inch till he got a second vocal signal. The more tightly the rope was bound, the more freedom the roof-walker felt. It was the bond that set him free.[17]

We sweat for wages but a gift is free. One is gotten by achieving; the other is received by believing (Rom. 6:23).

---

66 In his monumental masterpiece, historian Arnold Toynbee suggested that all human history expounds the text: "the wages of sin is death."[18]

Sooner or later we all sit down to a banquet of consequences.
—R. L. Stevenson, in Halford Luccock, *In the Minister's Workshop*

The wages of sin is death, but the gift of God is eternal life in Christ Jesus our Lord. —Paul (Romans 6:23)

6

ON THE TORTURE RACK

Romans 7

The shrill sound of police whistles of the London bobbies pierced the air as the chase was underway. The villainous Mr. Hyde was the object of the bobbies' chase.

Robert Louis Stevenson's *The Strange Story of Dr. Jekyll and Mr. Hyde* penetrates to great depths in its insight about human nature. Dr. Jekyll is the kindly physician known by all for his gentle reputation. But by chemical experimentation he turns himself into the deformed, malicious Mr. Hyde. With the passage of time, however, Mr. Hyde emerges from Jekyll's frame without any chemical inducement. Mr. Hyde has won out over Dr. Jekyll.

The subject of Stevenson's story is a two-in-one person. It is as if two persons were alive within the one body. Hyde prevails over Jekyll. What human being has not felt that way when the tug-of-war over good and evil escalates within? As if we were clamped inside some ancient torture rack, we feel we are being torn apart from both sides.

This tug of war is the subject of the tension-filled Romans 7. It's like an autobiographical excerpt clipped from Paul's own journal.

Newlyweds (Rom. 7:1-6)

As master-illustrator, Paul portrayed the Christian in Romans 7:1-6 as a newlywed. Yet we find that the term "law" is referred to almost 80 times in Romans. The classical scholar J. B. Lightfoot argued that "the law" in parenthesis in Romans 7:1 must mean the civil law for his Roman readers. Thus, the analogy the apostle applied in verses 2 and 3 involved the *bindingness* of marriage. "By law a married woman is bound to her husband as long as he is alive" (7:2). Death dissolves the marriage relationship and allows another marriage. Christians can claim to be "married to another, even to him who is raised from the dead [that is, Christ]" (7:4, KJV).

In Romans 7:5 Paul spoke of being "in the flesh." In Paul's writing the term "flesh" frequently has a different meaning than what we might expect. "Flesh" may mean:

(1) the pinchable, soft-textured material underneath human skin;

(2) a synonym for human beings (Rom. 3:20; I Cor. 1:29);

(3) human nature governed by sin.

Obviously, its use in Romans 7:5 (and in 8:4-8) refers to human beings in their sinful condition apart from Christ. Operating in this "flesh" (that is, in the non-Christian) are the "sinful passions." These passions operate "in our bodies" (7:5).

In verse 6 Paul shifted from the way "we were" (7:5) to the Christian's condition "now." Now we are "freed by death from our imprisonment" (7:6, Jerusalem Bible). Now we can serve "not in the old way, mechanically obeying a set of rules" (Living Bible), but "in the new way of the Spirit."

Ω The Greek word for "spirit" (KJV) does not automatically tell a translator whether the first letter should be capitalized or not. In most of the ancient Greek manuscripts, all words began with lowercase letters. A person must judge whether "spirit" means the human spirit or the Holy Spirit from each context where the word appears.

Sinai and Sin (Rom. 7:7-12)

We *died* to sin— 6:2; and
We *died* to the Law—7:4.
(Therefore? Do we have a syllogism?)
Is the Law sin? (Rom. 7:7).

54

What is the relationship between Sinai and sin? The apostle answers his own question—and he appears to answer it autobiographically (for there are seven first person pronouns ["I" or "me"] in 7:7-12). He burrows into his own being and psychoanalyzes his own thought processes.

? What kinds of discoveries have you made about yourself by self-examination?

The Law was responsible for consciousness raising. "Just as the sun's rays call forth the possibilities that are in the seed and bring them to full growth, so the law calls forth the sin that slumbers."[1] Leslie Allen observed: "Significantly the one commandment that defeated Paul was the tenth [Ex. 20:17 in Rom. 7:7], the one that concerns an inner attitude and not externals."[2]

" The earth is a nursery in which men and women play at being heroes and heroines, saints and sinners; but they are dragged down from their fool's paradise by their bodies.
—George Bernard Shaw, in Stuart Babbage, *Man in Nature and Grace*

Perhaps Paul—as many a teenage boy—had become aware of his newly awakened sex urges. Previously, he may have felt that he had sin (as defined in the Ten Commandments) pretty well corralled. Perhaps he felt somewhat snug and smug about this. No big problems with stealing or murder. But what about that fatal Tenth Commandment: "You must not have evil desires in your heart" (LB)?

Sin was the sleeping lion in Paul. As long as sin was dormant, Paul was unaware of its existence in him. Nevertheless, the "law excites and incites sin to more aggravated transgression."[3]

In a sermon, Hal Lindsey told about a new luxury motel going up along the beach in Galveston, Texas. The motel manager figured, "People are going to assume they can fish off of the balconies and heavy, lead sinkers will break our windows." Consequently, he had signs printed up to read: NO FISHING OFF BALCONIES. Some 40 windows were broken out during the first week! But when he took the written prohibition down, interestingly, the window-breakage began to diminish.

"One Paris printer rushed through an edition of 24,000 copies of Erasmus' Colloquies on hearing a rumor that the Sorbonne was about to condemn it."[4]

The reality is the good Law stimulates sin, which is bad. Hence, sin uses the Law to set up a beachhead of operation within us. But the problem is with our internal corruption and not with the external commandments ("the law is holy, and the commandment is holy, righteous and good" 7:12).

Is Law the Outlaw? (Rom. 7:13, 14)

The Great Debate—that might be a good title for Romans 7:13-25 as far as Bible commentators are concerned—for there is no unanimous agreement about the spiritual condition of the individual referred to in this section. Does it refer to Paul under the Law before his conversion? Or does the struggle of these verses characterize Paul the Christian? This is one of the more hotly debated theological questions in the Scriptures.

Some commentators argue from verses 7-13 that Paul is recalling his Jewish *bar mitzvah* when, as a young man, he became acutely sensitized to the fact that his sin went beyond the lack of outward conformity to the Law (7:7). Thus, George Turner said, "The struggle with indwelling sin in Romans 7 is not the description of the normal 'saint' but rather the futility of justification by Law, apart from Christ."[5] By contrast, Augustine, Calvin, and Luther accepted these verses as a description of Christian experience.[6] Others have concluded it is neither preconversion or normal Christian experience, but a believer who isn't appropriating the "law of the Spirit of life" of Romans 8:2.

Some make a point of pointing out that a transition occurs between 7:7-13 and 7:14-25 in that Paul shifted from the past tense to the present tense. Therefore, a number believe that verses 14-25 mark a converted state.

No matter which particular perspective on this passage one adopts, there is a chime that rings true here inside both non-Christians and Christians. Even conscientious non-Christians, wrestling with temptation, can identify with the tension felt here. Likewise, most candid Christians admit that there have been times, too, when they have felt like these verses were a paradigm of their Christian experience.

From a traditional Jewish viewpoint of that day Paul seemed to be drawing a bead on the Law, like some crack marksman taking aim at sitting ducks. The imaginary opponent (upon hearing Rom. 7:5, 7, and 11) might logically ask: Are you saying that the Law is bad? Is it the real culprit?

One might draw the wrong conclusion from Paul that the Law was a villain (from 7:5, 7, and 11). The Living Bible paraphrases Romans 7:13—"Didn't the law cause my doom? How then can it be good? No, it was sin, devilish stuff that it is." The Law is a magnifying glass, so that sin is seen as sin (7:13). As if sin were a criminal paraded out in a police lineup, sin is exposed to be exactly what it is—sin. Because of the Law, it is "recognized as sin." Mandarin chocolate ice cream is just about the chocolatiest chocolate one can buy—it is exceedingly chocolaty. Likewise the Law shows sin as "exceeding[ly] sinful" (7:13, KJV). It is as if the wrestler's mask is pulled off of Sin the Villain, and is publicly exposed.

THE CULPRIT
In a Peanuts cartoon, Charlie Brown appears before Lucy's psychiatric stand. Lucy says to him, "Discouraged again, Charlie Brown?" She continues, "The trouble with you is that you're you." Charlie responds in the next frame, "What in the world can I do about that?" Lucy's answer is, "I don't pretend to give advice; I merely point out the trouble." Therefore, Lucy and the apostle agree—the trouble with us is that we're us.

The 'I's Have It (Rom. 7:15-20)

Alva McClain made this vital statistical observation: "From verse 7 to the end of the chapter, the personal pronoun *I* occurs 30 times! The personal pronoun *me* occurs 12 times; the personal pronoun *my* occurs

4 times . . . . 47 times the personal pronoun occurs in 19 verses."[7] Yes, the "I"s (not "ayes") have the vote in this chapter—and there is a severe "I" (not "eye") problem.

Socrates said, "Men will do right, if they only know the right."[8] But the ancient Roman writer Ovid spoke more accurately than Socrates about human nature when he said, "I see and approve the better life, but I follow the worse one."[9] Certainly, Paul subscribed to Ovid's view rather than that of Socrates. "Some have been convinced, from this verse alone, [Rom. 7:15] that Paul was a golfer."[10]

REVERSE, PERVERSE PSYCHOLOGY

Sammy Baugh was a star quarterback for 16 seasons with the professional Washington Redskins. Despite having helped his former college team win two post-season bowl games, Sammy had come to TCU on a baseball scholarship. In fact, he wanted to play professional baseball, since he figured "he wouldn't last more than 2 or 3 years in pro football." Baugh was a low draft pick in football. Yet, he was told, "Play for me this fall for the highest paycheck a player ever got, plus a bonus for signing. Then, if you want, you can try baseball next spring." Sammy helped the Redskins football team win the championship in his rookie season.

Nevertheless, Sammy Baugh the football player wanted to be Sammy Baugh the baseball player. In the spring of 1938 he tried to make the St. Louis Cardinals baseball team but failed. Baugh might have borrowed Romans 7:15—"What I want to do I do not do, but what I hate I do." He seemed to be a walking case of reversed psychology.

In the New Yorker magazine this poem was found, somewhat illustrating Paul's feelings:

> Here a little child I stand,
> Holding up my either hand;
> One is dirty, one is clean,
> I'm the problem in between.

Paul finds himself at odds with himself (7:15), providing in verses 15-20 his own commentary on the expression "sold . . . to sin" in verse 14. Since his acted-out desires don't match his designs, it is a roundabout way of owning that "the law is good" (7:16).

Because his best blueprints go awry, Paul digs deeper to the real culprit—"sin living in me" (7:17). He has an alien lodger as a tenant.

Keith Miller echoed the apostle Paul when he wrote, "Inside, my soul was like a tableau of warriors by Michaelangelo, the figures twisting and turning for release."[11]

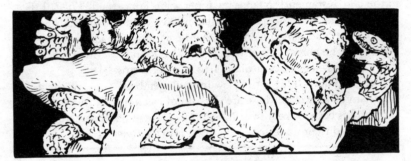

Paul's plans were at odds with his performance (7:18). His desires didn't jibe with his "do"s (7:19). Like Pilate who pronounced Christ innocent but went on and executed him, we rationally consent to what is right, yet we fail to pull off our resolutions.[12]

 THE WAR WITH OUR WILLS
"No one commends chastity more forthrightly than does Shakespeare in a famous passage in The Tempest; yet Shakespeare himself 'had,' as we say, 'to be married.' [John] Howard, the humanitarian prison-reformer, publicly advocated the practice of charity, nevertheless Howard at home was a tyrant. [The Scottish poet Robert] Burns describes happy home-life but was no 'model of husbandly or fatherly behavior'."

—Ian Macpherson, The Burden of the Lord

The War of the Worlds of 'Law's (Rom. 7:21-25)

Some years back, one Christian organization published an evangelistic pamphlet called "The Four Spiritual Laws." In verses 21-25 Paul sets forth his own version of four spiritual laws. They are:

(1) the law of sin (the "law," of vs. 21);
(2) the Law of Scripture ("God's law," vs. 22);
(3) the "law . . . within my members" (vs. 23); and
(4) "the law of my mind" (vs. 23).

The term "law" in all but the second case means a "principle" (as in the "law" of gravity).

Theologian James Denney commented on Romans 7:21—"To be saved from sin a man must at the same time own it and disown it; it is this practical paradox which is reflected in this verse."[13]

The first law (vs. 21) pinpoints this principle of moral gravity. He wants to soar, but the downdrag of sin keeps him sin-prone and habit-bound. We have called this the law of sin.

The second Law we have labeled the Law of Scripture, for Paul acknowledged: "I am in hearty agreement with God's Law [embodied in the Old Testament] so far as my inner self is concerned" (7:22, J. B. Phillips). Like an art judge whose hands have been amputated, he can pick *out* the blue ribbon paintings, but he cannot pick *up* what he approves. The phrase "inner being" (7:22) is found two other places in Paul's epistles—at II Corinthians 4:16 and Ephesians 3:16.

The third law (7:23) is the "law in [my] members" (i.e., physical parts). In other words, these are the "sinful passions" (7:5) operating through his body. Like a swirling whirlpool, these have tremendous suction, and their undertow brings him into captivity (7:23).

Christina Rosetti captured Paul's predicament poetically:[14]

> Myself, arch-traitor to myself;
> My hollowest friend, my deadly foe,
> My clog whatever road I go.

> Yet one there is can curb myself,
>> Can roll the strangling hold from me,
> Break off the yoke and set me free.

Charles Wesley wrote:[15]

> My strong propensity to ill,
>> My carnal mind and crooked will
> To only evil prone.
>> My downward appetite I find,
> My spirit, soul, and flesh inclined
>> To earth, and earth alone.

The fourth law of our spiritual Isaac Newton is "the law of my mind (7:23; cf. 7:25). If this law were the only law, the inner tension might seem to be at an end, but alas . . . .

It is this war of the worlds of the four laws that catapults the wrenching cry of verse 24 from him: "Who will rescue me from this body of death?" Some have claimed that Paul drew his picture from a barbaric practice of some brutal enemies who tied a corpse around the body of offenders.

In this section of chapter 7 the only glimmer of relief and release from the apparently insurmountable dilemma appears in the escape-words "through Jesus Christ our Lord." Like some Jeremiah enclosed in an unclimbable cistern with mud-slick perpendicular walls, Paul reveals the ropes of his Rescuer—only to enlarge this subject in chapter 8.

CHAPTER
7

BEYOND SIN'S GRAVITATIONAL PULL

Romans 8

The billing under the lights reads: "The Masked Marauder Rasslin' Mr. Clean." The Masked Marauder is your professional meanie, with hooded head, who shouts menacing taunts at the blond, statuesque wrestler with rippling muscles in the other corner. The crowd loves it.

The scenario is pretty familiar—the villain wrestling against "the good guy." Each one wins a round before the Marauder resorts to illegal tactics and antics and the real roughhouse stuff starts. If the bad guy wins, there'll be a return grudge match. But the unwritten rule of the wrestling show circuit dictates that Mr. Clean must win in the end.

Romans 8 also opens with a square-off: the flesh versus the Spirit. In Romans 7 the villain ("flesh") appeared to have the upper hand, but that's where the bell sounds as Romans 8 opens.

Both Romans and Galatians focus on the subject of justification by faith. Besides that, there are a number of overlapping themes, some of which are charted below.

	ROMANS 8	GALATIANS
The Law	vs. 3	3:5-22
Walking in the Spirit	vs. 4	5:25
Flesh versus Spirit	vss. 5-8	5:19-25
Slaves versus Sons	vss. 15, 16	3:23-4:7
Bondage	vs. 15	4:9
Spirit cries "Abba, Father"	vs. 15	4:6

Galatians 3—5, then, is a helpful cross-reference to numerous subjects in Romans 8.

Peanut Butter and Okra (Rom. 8:1-8)

Have you ever eaten a peanut butter and okra sandwich? Probably not. The two don't really go together—one sticks and the other squishes and slides. Neither are the "flesh" and the "Spirit" compatible. They carry on an unceasing warfare, because "they that are in the flesh cannot please God" (Rom. 8:8, KJV). By "flesh" Paul is not talking about the soft, pinchable matter covering our bones, but our very selves viewed from a sinful, selfish standpoint.

The following outline may help you in unlocking this first secion of Romans 8.

"Who will rescue me?" (Rom. 7:24)
 I. The fact of our deliverance enunciated (8:1)
II. The form of our deliverance explained (8:2-11)
  A. Delivered from "the law of sin" (8:2-4)

B. Delivered from "the law of . . . death" (8:2, 5-11)
   1. From spiritual death (8:5-10)
   2. From physical death (8:11)

In Romans 8 the Holy Spirit is named no less than 19 times. In Romans 8:1-8 Paul offers three reasons for not living a life geared around and regulated by our sinful selves. First, in vss. 1 and 3, Paul indicates that the sinful life-style stands condemned by God's sending His Son. If God sent His Son for the purpose of making sin unemployed and we continue sinning, then we are undermining the very purpose for which Christ came.

Because Christ came, Charles Wesley could sing:

> No condemnation now I dread;
> Jesus and all in Him is mine.

Paul asserts "There is now no condemnation" (8:1). F. F. Bruce wrote that "there is no reason why those . . . in Christ Jesus . . . should go on . . . as though they had . . . never been liberated from the prison-house of sin."[1]

 CHARRED GROUND AT CALVARY

In the early days of pioneer settlement in the western United States, one of the feared dangers was a great prairie fire. A settler might have worked for months building a log cabin only to see his labors destroyed by a consuming prairie fire. Practically the only way to combat a prairie fire was by counterattack. The settler could set a backfire in the grassy area immediately around the house and burn out a protective circle. Then, as the marauding prairie fire swept relentlessly toward the little log cabin, it would halt at the burned-off circle. The prairie grass only burned once.

There is sheltered soil at Mount Calvary. As Major Andre wrote of Christ:

> On Him almighty judgment fell
>   Which must have sunk a world to hell.
> He bore it for a sinful race,
>   And so became our hiding place.

Because God "made him [i.e., Christ] . . . to be sin [i.e., a sin-offering] for us" (II Cor. 5:21), "there is now no condemnation for those who are in Christ Jesus" (Rom. 8:1). There is charred ground at Calvary.

Not only does Paul assert the no-condemnation condition of those who "are in Christ Jesus," he also explains why that condition exists and what we can become in verses 2-4. There is "no condemnation" because of what the Spirit has done (vs. 2) and what the Son has done (vs. 3).

Secondly, our lives need not be ruled and regulated by sin because the Spirit enables us to live by a different principle (Rom. 8:2, 4). "Moses' law has right but not might; sin's law has might but not right'; the law of the Spirit has both might and right."[2] Concerning "sin and death" (8:2), A. Skevington Wood stated: "The twin tyrants of sin and death are deprived of their dictatorship."[3] These were the very words echoed at Aldersgate in John Wesley's crisis experience: "I felt my heart strangely warmed, I felt I did trust in Christ, Christ alone, for salvation; and an assurance was given me, that He had taken away my sins, even mine, and saved me from the law of sin and death." The "law of sin and death" (8:2) is like the down-tug to earth of the law of gravity. But the law of gravity can be overcome by the laws of flight. And the "law of the Spirit of life" (8:2) overcomes "the law of sin."

Paul moves from what he does not seem to be able to do in verse 2 to "what the law could not do" (KJV) in verse 3 (read 7:7-14 to see what he means). Weymouth's translation refers to the power of God's Law "thwarted as it was by human fraility." Yet, it was in the very fraility of the human condition that Christ came (8:3). God did through His Son what humanity had been unable to do even while possessing God's Law. Stuart Briscoe noted that the Law had the same problem that his grade school music teacher had had with that class of children—"he, like the law, although brilliant, was weak through our flesh."[4]

"There is now no condemnation" (8:1) because "God . . . condemned sin in sinful man" (i.e., in the very arena where sin had set up its headquarters, 8:3) through the deathblow dealt it in the death of Christ. Verse 3 explores *how* Christ came, and verse 4 explains *why* Christ came. Christ's death was "for sin," which may mean "as a sin-offering" (as it frequently does in the Greek version of the Old Testament, called the Septuagint [sep-TWO-uh-jint]). Just as the vaccination scar marks the spot where the inoculating serum has been injected, even so Calvary marks the spot where Christ was made "to be sin for us (II Cor. 5:21).

The objective in Christ's dying (vs. 3) was that it might result in the right kind of living (vs. 4) by us. The righteous results that the Law had aimed at all along find fulfillment in the Spirit-animated life. Augustine said: "Grace was given that the law might be fulfilled."

A third reason our lives should not be regulated by sinfulness is that the sinful life ("the flesh") is utterly opposed to God (Rom. 8:5-8). "The flesh is the life of the I for itself."[5] The flesh and Spirit have an opposite outlook ("set their minds on" [NASB], vs. 5), an opposite outcome ("death" versus "life," vs. 6), and an entirely opposite orientation altogether (vss. 7 and 8).

The poet Tersteegen summarized the two poles in Romans 8:5-8 by writing:

> Man earthy, of the earth, an hungered feeds
> On earth's dark poison tree—
> Wild gourds and deadly roots, and bitter weeds;
> And as his food is he.
> And hungry souls there are, that find and eat
> God's manna day by day;
> And glad they are, their life is fresh and sweet,
> For as their food are they!
> —in W. R. Newell's *Romans, Verse by Verse*

The Up-Puller (Rom. 8:9-14)

Paul informed his Roman readers: you are "in the Spirit" and the Spirit is "in you" (8:9). If, however, the Spirit of God unites with the spirit of a Christian, what about the body? The body still dies (vs. 10b). As the French commentator Godet put it, the body "begins to die the instant it begins to live."[6] Nevertheless, within the husk of the believer's body is planted the kernel of the Spirit. The Spirit is the tenant within (vs. 9b). If this "Spirit is life" (KJV) He will raise Christian's bodies up in the future (8:11) and He will raise Christians in their life-styles in the present (8:12-14).

 WHAT'S WITHIN?
Skevington Wood wrote: "Just as the royal standard above Buckingham Palace indicates that the queen is in residence, so the mark of the Spirit bears witness to the fact that the King" is within.[7]

The late renowned preacher Donald Grey Barnhouse approached the same issue from another analogy: "An electrical bulb may be screwed into the socket and the current turned on, but if there is no filament within the bulb, there will be no light."[8]

In verse 9 we are forced to conclude that Paul's term "flesh" (KJV) means vastly more than "body." Paul could not possibly say to his readers, "ye are not in the flesh" (KJV, meaning "body"; otherwise, he would be saying that they were a bunch of bodiless spirits. And it's hard to write letters to those folks!).

The New English Bible renders 8:9b clearly: "if [one] does not possess the Spirit of Christ, he is no Christian." Thus, one definition of a Christian is he or she is someone in whom God's Spirit is living. By the same token (because of the parallel structure of verses 9 and 10) we learn that "if the Spirit of God lives in you" (vs. 9), then "Christ is in you" (vs. 10). This passage is one of the clearest New Testament references to the in-living Spirit and in-living Christ.

However, although Christians possess the living Spirit, they also possess dying "mortal" bodies (8:11). In verse 11 we come to the longest title of the Holy Spirit in the New Testament. By contrast, verse 11 is the second and only other place where single title "Jesus" is used, the other being 3:26.[9] In fact, all three members of the Trinity are clustered in verse 11—(1) "the Spirit," (2) "him," i.e., God the Father, and (3) "Christ." The Father is the source and the Spirit is the means of the resurrection of believers' bodies in verse 11. The same Spirit who has come down to live within a believer's body will one day raise up that body.

A Believer's Baby Talk (Rom. 8:15-17)

A CHART OF CONTRASTS

spirit of slavery (8:15)	"Spirit of sonship" (8:15)
brings back to bondage	breathes out in boldness
cringing and cowardice	confidence and conviction
views God as Punisher	views God as Parent

The sons of God pray as the Son of God prayed (Mk. 14:36)—"Abba, Father" (8:15).

Dr. Allan MacRae, seminary president, had to be away from home for several weeks after his baby was born. Upon returning home, his little son stretched out his arms and said, "Ab-Abba!" Dr. MacRae, a scholar of ancient Near Eastern languages, said, "Look, he's speaking Aramaic already!"[10] Abba was the Aramaic equivalent for da-da, a child's word for its daddy. What an ouster of formalism!

> My God is reconciled;
> His pardoning voice I hear.
> He owns me for His child;
> I need no longer fear.
> With confidence I now draw nigh,
> And "Father, Abba, Father" cry.
> —Charles Wesley

> "What is the alchemy which converts the lead of conviction into the gold of divine confidence? The answer is the testimonium of the Spirit."
> —Bernard Ramm, *The Witness of the Spirit*

The Three Groans (Rom. 8:18-27)

The Three Groans is not the name of a modern rock band. Rather, it is a summary of Romans 8:18-27, for:
   (1) "the . . . creation has been groaning" (8:22);
   (2) "we [Christians] groan inwardly" (8:23); and
   (3) "the Spirit . . . groans" (8:26).

This is surely the most important of all the passages that expound upon the renewing of Creation.

> Dr. Robert Schaper was leading prayer in seminary chapel after reading the panegyric on creation in Psalm 19. He prayed, "Lord, the world of creation speaks to us audibly if we have ears to hear." Just as he was praying, the blaring, glaring wail of an ambulance siren passing by almost drowned him out. It was as if the truth of Romans 8 had overridden the truth of Psalm 19—creation was groaning.
>
> Similarly, a Humanities class of Mrs. Bentley, at Bryan College, was listening to the phonographic marvels of a Beethoven classic. Simultaneously, down the outside corridor maneuvered a student who was forced to walk with Canadian crutches. *Scrape-scrape-scrape* . . . the grating, rasping sound seemed to turn the symphony into cacophany!

Nature "sighs and throbs in pain."[11] It is as if creation were experiencing the wrenching contractions of childbirth. It is as if nature "feels in her womb the leaping of a new universe."[12]

> How is it with old mother-earth? Is she full of the glory of God? [She is] a poor, withered, wrinkled thing hidden in powders and cosmetics.
> —John H. Jowett, *God Our Contemporary*

Ω Nevertheless "the creation waits in eager expectation" (8:19). Skevington Wood commented that the Greek word "indicates a straining forward, like crowds at a stadium as the competitors speed past. Literally, it is 'watching with outstretched head.' " J. B. Phillips renders the phrase colorfully: "The whole creation is on tiptoe to see the wonderful sight of the sons of God coming into their own."

Not only does creation groan (8:18-22), but Christians groan, too, (8:23-25). We are waiting to be "glorified" (8:30), i.e., to receive "the redemption of our bodies" (8:23). Thus, we live in tension (see chart).

past event	prospective expectation
"did . . . receive" (8:15)	"we wait" (8:23)
—already accomplished	—awaited with anticipation
adoption	glorification
"a spirit" (8:15)	"our bodies" (8:23)

Ω We "have the firstfruits of the Spirit" (8:23). The barley harvest preceded the wheat harvest in Israel. On the day following Sabbath, at Passover, a green sheaf of barley (called the "Firstfruits") was waved before the Lord (Lev. 23:9, 10). Waving the first ripened grain was a way of broadcasting: There's more to come. Better things are yet to be!

> Blessed assurance; Jesus is mine;
> Oh, what a foretaste of glory divine.

The same Greek word translated "firstfruits" is the word used in modern Greek for an engagement ring.[13] The Holy Spirit is indeed the first installment of greater "glory that will be revealed in us" (8:18).

God's Chain Links (Rom. 8:28-30)

Many Christians misunderstand Romans 8:28 as if it were saying that only good things will happen to God's people. But some things that happen to us aren't good. Yet God is stirring them together for good. A cook takes flat-tasting flour, a stick of margarine, raw eggs (yukk!), and bitter chocolate—most of which taste unpleasant by themselves—and then "works" all those things together "for . . . good." After they emerge from the oven in the final product—a chocolate cake—they taste good. But the individual ingredients aren't mouth-watering at all.

C. S. Lewis said, "We are listening to a long symphony. If we only hear a few bars or measures we may hear dissonant sounds or cacophony." A few oboe notes or viola strains—if heard apart from the total symphony piece—probably wouldn't make much sense. Only the total blending of musical instruments produces the magnificent harmony of a symphony. All the instruments work together for good.

Jacob wailed in the Old Testament, "All these things are against me"(Gen. 42:36, KJV). And so it seemed at the time. Nevertheless, the great Scriptwriter had planned so that things worked together for good in the long haul concerning Jacob's life. So, the tapestry of a Christian's life is woven by the Master Weaver.

"Many years ago an eminent French engineer was detained in the Mediterranean by a tedious quarantine. It was hard . . . to endure such confinement, but as he waited on the deck of the vessel he read, and the book to which he gave extra attention prompted him to the conception of the Suez Canal . . . . Did M. de Lesseps afterwards regret those dragging days of quarantine?"[14]

Captain Scott and Edward Wilson were the only two finally left alive in the fateful Antarctic Expedition. Snowbound, one wrote: "To my beloved wife. Don't be unhappy—all is for the best. We are playing a good part in a great scheme arranged by God Himself, and all is well . . . . We will meet after death . . . . All is for the best to those that love God, and oh . . . we have both loved Him with our lives."[15]

Above are two tragedies. The man in the first was able to see past tragedy while still in this life. The other man possessed a rare, telescopically eternal perspective, believing that the tangled threads were but the backside of God's tapestry. Changing the imagery slightly:

> My life is but a weaving
> Between my Lord and me;
> I may not choose the colors,
> He knows what they should be;
> For He can view the pattern
> Upon the upper side,
> While I can see it only
> On this, the under side.
>
> Not till the loom is silent
> And the shuttles cease to fly
> Shall God unroll the canvas
> And explain the reason why—
> The dark threads are as needful
> In the Weaver's skillful hand
> As the threads of gold and silver
> In the pattern He has planned.

The pattern God weaves is "according to his purpose" (v. 28). Five chain links in God's plan are specified in verses 29 and 30:

1. foreknew;
2. predestined;
3. called;
4. justified; and
5. glorified.

Puritan John Owen said, "God's prevision is his provision."[16] In all five of the chain links God is the Agent, the Welder.

Super Conquerors in the Slaughterhouse (Rom. 8:31-37)

If "all things work together for good" (KJV) for believers, then verses 31-39 is a commentary on verse 28. Here's how this works out. Judging from verses 35 and 36, there were tension-filled times for the Roman readers. They are losers who are (paradoxically) winners.

"More than conquerors" (8:37) is actually one Greek word, found only here in the New Testament. But these Super Conquerors are not musclebound, imperturbable heroes in the comic book mold. Paul compares them (in a quote from Ps. 44:22) to sheep in the slaughterhouse (8:36). Theirs isn't a pretty picture. They didn't know if they'd be alive tomorrow. But it is these people in this decimated condition who are Super Conquerors. While their necks are on the chopping block, God brands them Super Conquerors.

To reinforce this point, Paul poses a questionnaire in verses 31-35, a battery of six rhetorical questions.

Ω In Romans 8:35 Paul listed seven theoretical severers from Christ's love. Donald Barnhouse stated of the word "trouble": "The English word comes from the Latin name for a flail: A piece of wood, a little longer than a broomstick has attached to it by leather thong a shorter piece of wood. The laborer swings the flail through the air and the shorter piece of wood beats upon the wheat, separating the grain from the chaff."[17]

Have you ever felt like you have undergone the harrowing experience of being flailed?

The next word in verse 35, "hardship," is no less picturesque, for the root meaning of the Greek word depicted a narrowness of space. It would carry the same feeling as our word "claustrophobia." Sometimes we feel like we are clamped inside a vice (for example, if we feel trapped in our job).

 IF THE GREATER, WHY NOT THE LESSER? (8:32)
A wealthy Roman had a son who broke his heart and a slave who commanded his admiration. He decided on his deathbed to disinherit his son and leave everything to this slave, Marcellus. He drew up the papers and called in his son to tell him what he had done. "I have deeded everything to the slave Marcellus," he said. "However, you may choose one item from my estate for yourself." "I'll take Marcellus!" was the son's reply. When we take Christ, we take all.[18]

Exalted Eloquence (Rom. 8:38, 39)

Erasmus, a famous late medieval scholar, exclaimed about these verses, "What has Cicero ever said more grandiloquently?" Yes, it is exhilarating eloquence which consummates this major section of Romans. W. E. Vine, in his commentary on the Book of Romans), following the same order of the text as the NIV and the best Greek manuscripts, points out the arrangement of verses 38 and 39:

a) neither death nor life (impersonal);
b) nor angels nor principalities (personal);

a) nor things present nor things to come (impersonal);
b) nor powers (personal);

a) nor height nor depth (impersonal);
b) nor any other creature (personal).

Vine calls this "the crowning arch of the whole epistle."

Jakob Spener is quoted as saying, "if Holy Scripture was a ring, and the Epistle to the Romans a precious stone, chapter 8 would be the sparkling point of the jewel."

—in Griffith Thomas, *St. Paul's Epistle to the Romans*

8

CAN THE JUSTIFIER BE JUSTIFIED?

Romans 9—11

Romans deals with the subject of *righteousness revealed*. But how can God be righteous and declare the unrighteous to be righteous (Rom. 3:26)? That is answered in Romans 1—8.

Question No. 2 is: How can God be righteous if He makes promises to His people, the Jews, and doesn't come through on them? That is the subject of Romans 9—11. Note that the very same issue applied to the individual in the early chapters (3:27, 28) is applied to Israel in the middle chapters (9:30-32). Romans 9—11 grapples with "the faithfulness of God and the failure of Israel."[1]

Soul Brothers (Rom. 9:1-5)

I. *The Righteousness of God is Vindicated (9:1-29).*

   A. Paul's Pathos and Israel's Past Privileges (9:1-5). Like Moses, who would sever himself from God for his people (Ex. 32), so Paul could wish himself severed rather than see his people severed (9:3). "I have actually reached the pitch of wishing myself cut off from Christ if it meant that they could be won for God" (J. B. Phillips).

When Disraeli became Lord Beaconfield, he was twitted in the House of Lords because of his Jewish ancestry. Disraeli replied, "Yes . . . I am a Jew, and when your ancestors were living on acorns in the German forest, my ancestors were giving to the world law, literature, religion, and our very Savior."[2]

In Romans 9:4, 5, Paul piles up eight stacks of stock in his Hebrew heritage. The pinnacle of these privileges is "Christ, who is God" (9:5). Although scholars debate whether this is the correct understanding, Weiss says that here the word God "can be referred only to Christ."[3] Richard Longnecker agreed that here Paul "explicitly identified Jesus as God."[4]

Now That's Choice! (Rom. 9:6-33)

    B. God's Righteous Choice Is Vindicated (9:6-13)
        1. In the choice of Isaac rather than Ishmael (9:6-9)
        2. In the choice of Jacob rather than Esau (9:10-13)

In both cases the choice came before the children were born (9:11).

    C. God's Righteous Character Is Vindicated (9:14-23).
        1. Is God unfair (9:14-18)? Look at Pharaoh.
        Notice the parallel:
            a. 9:15—"he [God] says to Moses," Exodus 33:19;
            b. 9:17—"the Scripture says to Pharaoh," Exodus 9:16.

In the first case God's "mercy" (9:15) is apparent; in the second case, God's might (9:17) is transparent.
        2. Is God unresistible (9:19-23)? Look at pottery.

Gregory of Nyassa (c. 330-395) said that "the sick must not prescribe to the doctor the manner of treatment."[5] For Gregory's physician, Paul substitutes the potter (9:20). The Berkeley Version renders the verse: "Who are you anyway, to talk back to God?"

This section (Rom. 9:6-24) is one where the two branches of theology—Calvinism and Arminianism—butt heads. Calvinism stresses more heavily God's choice, whereas Arminianism accents human choice as decisive. Some have considered this whole section of Scripture as the classic on predestination. Pharaoh and (certainly) pottery appear to be but pawns in this passage. Hence, Romans 9:22, 23 is used as a proof text for John Calvin's doctrine of double-barrelled predestination—that God has not merely elected some to salvation, but has elected others for destruction. Nevertheless, whereas 9:23 speaks decisively of "the objects of his mercy, whom he [God] prepared in advance for glory," 9:22 stops short of saying that God is the subject of "prepared." It merely mentions "the objects of his wrath—prepared for destruction." Therefore, such scholars as Ralph Martin assert that "there appears here no warrant for any dogma of predestination to damnation."[6]

| Ω | Regarding "preparing for destruction," Alva MacClain asked: "Does it say God did it? No, it does not say that . . . . The middle voice of the Greek means that man fits himself for destruction. God never does that."[7] |

D. God's Righteous Concern Is Vindicated for Both Jew and Gentile (9:24-29). God chose both Jews and Gentiles. To document this point, Paul marshals four Old Testament texts:
   1. 9:25—Hosea 2:23;
   2. 9:26—Hosea 1:10;
   3. 9:27, 28—Isaiah 10:22, 23; and
   4. 9:29—Isaiah 1:9.

II. *The Righteousness of Faith Is Validated (9:30—10:21).*
   A. Righteousness by Faith Is Being Received by Gentiles (9:30-33). The term "righteousness" crops up three times in 9:30, 31. Israel's pursuit of righteousness had become like a misguided missile. Isaiah 8:14 coupled with 28:16 (in Rom. 9:33) parks on the two directions—
      1. the stumblers in Israel ("Zion") and
      2. the trusters (who, for Paul, have become Gentiles).

How Not to Be Sincerely Wrong (Rom. 10:1-13)

   B. Righteousness by Faith Is Being Refused by Jews for Righteousness by Law (10:1-13). "The righteousness that comes from God" (10:3) causes us to flash back to Romans's thesis statement in 1:17—the "righteousness from God is . . . a righteousness that is by faith" (cf. 9:32; 10:3).

COMPARATIVE CHART

"righteousness from God" (3:22)	"righteousness . . . from God" (10:3)
"apart from law" (3:21)	"the end of the law" (10:4)
"to all who believe" (3:22)	"for everyone who believes" (10:4)

| 66 | Of all the stars which fell to earth with the mighty firmament-shaking experience of Paul's conversion, the law was the greatest.
—H. J. Holtzmann, in Skevington Wood, *Life by the Spirit* |

ROMANS 10:4

"The Santa Fe Trail . . . runs out to Los Angeles. If you want to get to Los Angeles, you take that road. But suppose . . . you could just be . . . transported and set right down in Los Angeles. Would you, after you got there, say, 'I must go back and come over this Santa Fe Trail? You are already there; Los Angeles is the end."[8]

Romans 9—11 is assuredly a mosaic or patchwork quilt of Old Testament quotation.

Romans 10:5—Leviticus 18:5

Romans 10:6-8—Deuteronomy 30:14

Romans 10:11—Isaiah 28:16

Notice the NIV's rendering of Romans 10:9 (in preference to the KJV). The New Testament is chocked full of creedlets, or mini-statements of belief (see Jn. 11:27; Acts 2:36; 9:20; 17:3; I Jn. 2:22; 4:2; 5:1, 5). Probably the shortest three word creed in the New Testament is: "Jesus is Lord" (cf. I Cor. 12:3). "Jesus is Lord" here means that Jesus is deity, bearing the Old Testament title of Lord or Yahweh (the Jews' covenant name for Lord). Everett Harrison observed: "When verse 13 is compared with verse 9, it becomes evident that the Lord of Joel 2:32 is being identified with the Lord Jesus Christ. This poses a problem for those who refuse to ascribe full deity to the Savior."[9]

C. Refusal Is Inexcusable for Israel, as Scripture from Six Passages Says (10:14-21).

Genealogy of the Gospel (Rom. 10:14-17)

Paul saw a genealogy in all this—if you will, a family tree of faith. We may sketch the imaginary genealogy as follows:

(1) great-great-grandparent—sending (vs. 15);

(2) great-grandparent—proclaiming (vs. 14c);

(3) grandparent—hearing (vs. 14b);

(4) parent—believing (vs. 14a);

(5) child—calling (vs. 13).

"All these are steps in a ladder which stands amidst the welter of man's sin and ruin, its top lost in the glories of the Eternal City."[10] The airtight logic flows from what a kind of chain-syllogism in which each question backs up and retraces part of the one that came before it.[11] William Barclay said, "There is a kind of telegraphic quality about the writing [here]." [12]

WITHOUT A PREACHER (10:14)

"Sir Frederick Treves, the Royal Surgeon, was once travelling in a train which was involved in a railway accident. The driver and fireman were pinned beneath wreckage. Before long they . . . laid out . . . two sorely battered and unconscious bodies. . . . They turned . . . to the great surgeon . . . 'Sir, can you do anything?' Sir Frederick Treves . . . [said] 'Yes, I could save them—but I haven't got my instruments.' "[13]

After four questions in a row (in Romans 10:14, 15a) Paul proceeded to parade out six quotations in a row from the Old Testament. The parade consists of: Isaiah 52:7 (vs. 15b); Isaiah 53:1 (vs. 16); Psalm 19:4 (vs. 18); Deuteronomy 32:21 (vs. 19); Isaiah 65:1 (vs. 20); and Isaiah 65:2 (vs. 21).

A Celestial Conundrum (Rom. 11)

III. *Rejection and Its Results (11:1-36).*

    A. Abandoned by God? Remember the Remnant (11:1-10). Paul's mind was like a sponge soaked in the Old Testament. Regarding Romans 11:1-10, "At no other point in his letters does Paul cite the Old Testament text as much as he does here. . . . In 11:1-6 . . . 39 out of 105 words occur as quotation of the Old Testament (i.e., 37 percent). In 11:7-10 . . . 45 out of 75 words are Scripture (63 percent)."[14]

Ralph Martin outlined Romans 11:1-15 as follows:[15]

- The rejection of the Jews is partial, not complete (1-10)
- The rejection of the Jews is only temporary, not final (11-15)

J. B. Phillips phrased the question posed by Paul in 11:1, "This leads naturally to the question, 'Has God then totally repudiated his people?' " Was Israel an orphan? Since Israel was rejecting the Gospel, did that mean God would irrevocably reject Israel? Here, in a sense, God must explain himself. Does Israel's apostasy mean God's abandonment? No! Paul himself was case study number one to prove the contrary (11:1b). The apostle's answer encourages us never to write off anyone—no matter how Gospel resistant they may seem.

WE NEVER QUITE KNOW

David faithfully visited the home for delinquent boys. He attempted to get to know them, teach them, and demonstrate his Christian concern to them. But then the time came for him to move to another part of the country, so he had to say farewell to the boys.

One boy had hardly said anything during the time that David had visited in the home. Judging by the blank stare regularly on that boy's face, all David's efforts had been in vain. As David was walking for the last time down a long corridor that led to the home's exit, that boy appeared at the other end of the corridor and called, "I will miss you." That was all he said before he disappeared.

David never forgot those words—"I will miss you." If he had not heard them, he would never have believed that his message and life had made an impression on that boy.

We may never know how many people we are influencing for Christ. Paul cites Deuteronomy 29:4 and Isaiah 29:10 (Rom. 11:8) and Psalm 69:22, 23 (Rom. 11:9, 10) to show that some were hardened.

The noun behind the verb for "hardened" in 11:7 is *porosis* (cf. 11:25). As a medical term in Greek, it referred to the callus that hardened around a fracture, enabling the bone structure to mend.

Concerning the NIV's "stupor" in 11:8, F. F. Bruce noted that it "literally means 'pricking' or 'stinging' and hence comes to be used also of the numbness which results from certain kinds of stings."[16]

B. Advantages for Gentiles Through Guilt of Jews (11:11-15). The question in verse 1 led to another question in verse 11: "Now I ask myself, 'Was this fall of theirs an utter disaster?' " (J. B. Phillips). Again Paul gave a positive negative: "Far from it" (NEB). Success had sprung like a serendipity (or happy surprise) out of failure. The liability for the Jews became the asset of the Gentiles.

Paul hoped for a boomerang effect—that the rejection of the Good News generally by Jews and the reception of the Good News by Gentiles might spark and stimulate Jews to desire what the Gentiles had received. Paul argued from the lesser to the greater in 11:12.

C. Analogies Give Alarm (11:16-24). Paul used the analogy of (1) the lump of "dough offered as firstfruits" (11:16; see Num. 15:17-21), and (2) the grafting of "a wild olive shoot" (11:17-

24). The engrafted shoots (the Gentiles) were enjoying the enrichment of the original roots. Despite the fact that Gentiles generally were enjoying the place of privilege, Paul announced, "God is able to graft them [Jews] in again" (11:23).

D. Agenda for Jews Yet (11:25-29). The phrase in 11:26 ("all Israel will be saved") has been a pesky one for interpreters. Those called amillennialists generally hold that the term "Israel" is here elasticized (see "Jew" in Rom. 2:28) to include Gentiles (cp. Gal. 6:16; I Pet. 2:4-10 where Gentiles apparently assume Israel's descriptions and duties). Those called premillennialists often hold that "Israel" in 11:26 really does refer to a massive future conversion of literal Jews.

Compare quotations from three orthodox scholars below:
- Amillennialist William Hendriksen said: "all Israel" = "the entire believing remnant throughout all the ages."[17]
- E. M. Blaiklock wrote: "Observe that Paul cannot mean that all Jews, regardless of rebellion, will be saved. He must mean the 'new Israel,' the sum of the redeemed. Let verse 26 mean the Spiritual Israel, and the whole pattern of doctrine works to a proper conclusion."[18]
- F. F. Bruce holds that: "The large-scale conversion of the Gentile world is to be followed by the large-scale conversion of Israel," but "in all that Paul says about the restoration of Israel to God, he says nothing about the restoration of an earthly Davidic kingdom, nothing about national reinstatement in the land of Israel."[19]

Dispensationalists believe this refers to a regathering of national Israel in the end times when there will be a mass turning to Messiah.

E. Ascription of Adoration to God (11:30-36). The apostle's upsurge of adoration in Romans 11:33-36 is like a spiritual eagle soaring upward "with eyes wide open to the mercies of God" (12:1, J. B. Phillips). What a wonderful doxology this is! The Living Bible exclaims, "Oh, what a wonderful God we have! How great are his wisdom and knowledge and riches!" (11:33).

On St. Thomas in the Virgin Islands there is a grouping of aquariums called Coral World. One can go down 15 feet below the surface of the sea and get a glimpse of the depths of the ocean floor.

> We only see a little of the ocean,
>   A few miles distant from the rocky shore,
> But out there beyond the eye's horizon
>   There's more.

Verses 34-36 contain two sets of triplets. The first triplets come in the three questions of verses 34 and 35:

> "Who knows the mind of the Lord?
>   Who has been his counsellor?
> Who has ever made a gift to him, to receive a gift in return?" (NEB).

No Daniel Boone has ever tracked the ways of God. No Kit Carson has ever trailblazed the paths of God's movements. Who shall we elect as God's advisory counsel (Rom. 11:34)? Silly question.

The second set of triplets is the trio of prepositions "of," "through," and "to" in verse 36. God is the source, course, and force of all things. One might say that the kickoff, game plan, and final gun in the game of life all have their focus in God.

"Theology is doxology (i.e., praise) or it is nothing at all."[20] What can the reader say after such a passage except to fall to his or her knees before God and exclaim, "How great Thou art!" No wonder Paul found himself, as a classic hymn puts it, "lost in wonder, love, and praise."

CHAPTER
9

A WALKING GODARCHY
ROMANS 12

In order to set Romans 12 within the framework of the rest of the book, this outline of Romans 12—16 is offered:

I. *Principles on Living As One Rightly Related to God (12, 13)*
   A. Personal Principles (12:1-21)
      1. Give yourself to God (12:1, 2)
      2. Give of your gifts (12:3-8)
      3. Give rather than concentrating on getting back at others (12:9-21)
   B. Political Principles (13:1-7)
   C. Public Principles (13:8-14)
      1. Love's relationship to law (13:8-10)
      2. Life-style that is Christian (13:11-14)
II. *Perspectives Where Two Groups Operate (14:1—15:21)*
   A. Gray Areas—How the Strong-conscienced Christian Is to Relate to the Sensitive-conscienced Christian (14:1—15:7)
   B. Gentiles and Jews (15:8-21)
III. *Particular Plans with Regard to the Roman Readers (15:22-33)*
   A. Paul Has Been Prevented (15:22-24)
   B. Poverty Program in Progress (15:25-27)
   C. Paul's Plans (15:28, 29)
   D. Prayer Pleas from Paul (15:30-33)
IV. *Postlude (16)*
   A. Phoebe's Commendation (16:1, 2)
   B. Paul's Greetings (16:3-16)

C. Peril Sounded (16:17-20)
D. Paul's Party's Greetings (16:21-24)
E. Praise in Conclusion (16:25-27)

Presenting Ourselves to God (Rom. 12:1, 2)

Anders Nygren claimed, "Chapters 12—13 [of Romans] contain the fullest exposition that we have of Paul's central view of the ethical life of the Christian."[1] "Many people say *therefore* when nothing has gone before. Paul doesn't do that."[2] What is the "therefore" there for (12:1)? It is a gatepost by which we swing back to the preceding context (11:33-36).

In Romans 12:1 Paul the Apostle becomes Paul the Beggar ("I beseech you," KJV). The ancient Archimedes said that if he could just get a fulcrum outside of the world, he could move the world. Likewise, Paul finds his leverage points in at least three motives:

(1) the beseeching of Paul;
(2) the brotherhood of believers;
(3) the bounties of God ("in view of God's mercy").

God "has, as it were, besieged us with His mercies, brought them up against us in countless number, built the bulwarks of His grace against our souls, poured a ceaseless cannonade of kindness in upon the breaches of our hearts."[3]

Interestingly, Paul begins not with a purely spiritual presentation of ourselves, but with the physical.

⊞ DIRECTED BODIES
In Oliver Cromwell's time, soldiers went to arrest members of the British parliament who were in hiding. When the elderly Speaker of Parliament was captured and asked where members were hiding, he replied, "I have no eyes to see, no ears to hear, no hands to move, no feet to walk and no mouth to speak, save as directed by Parliament."[4]

The apostle admonishes his audience:
"offer your bodies" sacrificially (vs. 1);
"do not conform" to pressuring patterns (vs. 2a);
"be transformed" mentally (vs. 2b).

A physical presentation is urged by Paul in verse 1 before a psychological presentation in verse 2. This total presentation is:
(1) sacrificial—"living sacrifices";
(2) spiritual—"pleasing to God";
(3) sane—"your reasonable service" (KJV).

Unlike those recently quivering animal sacrifices strapped to an Old Testament altar waiting to die, we are to present our bodies as *living* sacrifices to God (vs. 1). The English poet William Cowper understood the kind of withdrawal pains involved in becoming living sacrifices. He wrote:

> Habits are soon assumed, but when we strive
> To strip them off, 'tis being flayed alive.

? What insights or motivations can you share from personal experience about attempting to break some harmful habit?

"Don't let the world around you squeeze you into its own mould" is J. B. Phillips' classic rendering of the negative obligation in verse 2. The positive side of that coin is to "be transformed" (vs. 2). From the Greek word back of "transformed" we derive the English word "metamorphosis," reminding us of the caterpillar which undergoes metamorphosis (that is, a complete change) to become a beautiful butterfly.

Romans 12:1, 2 is calling for nothing less than a total turnover of our being to God—becoming a walking Godarchy.

" Every business organization should have a vice-president in charge of constant renewal.

—Dwayne Orton, in Norman Vincent Peale,
Enthusiasm Makes a Difference

If I believed that it were permitted to one man—and only one—in this generation to lead a life of complete consecration to God, I would live in every respect as though I believed myself to be that one.

—Jonathan Edwards

The secret is simply this: God has had all there is of me.

—General William Booth of the Salvation Army

If I have done anything for Christ in my generation, it is because I have given myself entirely to Christ . . . .   —F. B. Meyer

Perspective on Spiritual Gifts (Rom. 12:3-8)

Once we have given ourselves to God (vss. 1, 2), we must give our gifts to God (vss. 3-6a). A part of the renewing of the mind (vs. 2) is that one be not high-minded (vs. 3, KJV) about his or her abilities, but to function giftedly and servingly within the multi-gifted Body of Christ (vss. 4-6). Surely a part of the renewing of our minds (12:2) entails the way we think about ourselves (12:3). The word "humility" may be related to *humus* (ground or soil) implying that we are to be down to earth in the way we think about ourselves.[5]

Berkeley Mickelsen noted the play on words behind verse 3—"not to be high-minded beyond what is proper to mind . . . but to set one's mind for the purpose of being of a sound . . . mind."[6] This sound-minded, sane-minded Christian will be one who uses his or her gift to the benefit of Christ's Body. Therefore, verses 6-8 contain a representative list of spiritual gifts (compare I Cor. 12:27-30; Eph. 4:11 ; and I Pet. 4:10, 11).

There are two sets of ways of understanding the expression in verse 3—"in accordance with the measure of faith." One way is that of the Jerusalem Bible: "Each of you must judge himself soberly by the standard of the faith." Another approach is that of the Good News Bible: "judge yourself according to the amount of faith that God has given you." In the first case, faith is understood as an external standard (or belief); in the second it is viewed as an internal process (or believing).

A group of school children prepared a gift for their teacher. Each kindergarten child (with the help of room mothers) provided an outline of his or her hand on a 5-inch piece of fabric. All the little hands were then sewn together into a single whole—a quilt.[7] Like many handprints sewn together on a unified quilt, so Christ's Body—the Church—is composed of many gifted believers complementing each other.

Principles on Serving (Rom. 12:9-13)

Romans 12:9-21 may be outlined:[8]
   (1) Manifold manifestations (vss. 9-13);
   (2) Moral maxims (vss. 14-21).

Romans 12:9-13 is a kind of grab bag of qualities that make life run more smoothly. There are 13 telegraph-like statements here. Part of verse 9 acts like an umbrella, covering the material of these verses—"Hate what is evil; cling to what is good."

Love of people is to be love without pretension (vs. 9a) and must be based upon love of principles (vs. 9b).

Ω "Sincere" in 12:9 means literally "unhypocritical." From the Greek, *hypo* + *krites* refers to one "under a mask." Donald G. Barnhouse supplied background for the word: "The Greek theater had neither background nor scenery nor costumes; the actors carried masks, made with such [frozen facial] expressions that the audience could easily see whether the character was tragic, comic, or melodramatic."[9] Thus, the mother whose son is on drugs, who is trying to hide her pain from church friends by "putting on a happy face" may illustrate this falseness, all the while thinking that she is being Christian about it.

While verse 10 focuses on attitudes ("devoted," "honor"), verse 11 is gauged around motivated activity ("zeal," "fervor," "serving"). The Berkeley Version renders the middle clause of verse 11, "keeping spiritually aglow." English evangelist George Whitefield said of the Holy Club at Oxford: "Their hearts glowed with the love of God."[10] There are times when we need to take a stoker to the embers so as to be more fervent.

Emotional enthusiasm comes over into the "joyful" of verse 12. As in Colossians 1:11 the note of joy is counterbalanced by being "patient." Joy bubbles need to be tempered by evenly temperatured patience. A little child once gave this definition of patience: "It's waiting in a hurry." Tribulation breeds not only patience, but prayer (vs. 12).

The inner characteristics of verse 12 find outer manifestations in verse 13—"when God's children are in need, you be the one to help them out. And get into the habit of inviting guests home for dinner . . ." (LB). The church that bought a little girl an expensive hearing aid that she needed was exemplifying the first part of this verse. Helpful and hospitable—how we can use more of these traits!

Paul's 'Sermon on the Mount' (Rom. 12:14-21)

Compare Jesus' Sermon on the Mount and Paul's mini-version of it charted below.

JESUS	PAUL
Matthew 5:11	Romans 12:14
You are blessed when persecuted	Bless your persecutors
Matthew 5:44	Romans 12:44
Matthew 5:12—rejoice when persecuted	Romans 12:15a—rejoice with the rejoicing
Matthew 5:43, 44	Romans 12:17, 19-21

Interestingly, this same section begins with the word "bless" (vs. 14), echoing the keyword from the Beatitudes in Matthew 5—"blessed."

As a postscript, compare Romans 12:15 and James 5:13 where Paul extends the emotion beyond oneself to others. In one sense, this is but an extension of the Golden Rule. If I am to do to others as I would want them to do to me, then I will reflect the emotional mood I would want someone else to feel (whether rejoicing or weeping; Rom. 12:15). This will foster a harmonious mentality (12:16).

Another aspect of a Christlike mind-set is brought out by the J. B. Phillips rendering of Romans 12:16 ("Don't become snobbish but take a real interest in ordinary people. Don't become set in your own opinions").

It's one thing to live harmoniously with rejoicers or "ordinary people," it's another thing to obey verses 17-21. Justice would seem to be aborted when we are told not to pay back evil with evil (12:17).

The Living Bible paraphrases the second part of verse 17—"do things in such a way that everyone can see you are honest clear through." Transparent truthfulness (vs. 17) has as its purpose the promotion of peace (vs. 18). However, it is not peace at any price. Peace is profitable:

(1) if it can be managed ("if it is possible,") and

(2) if you can manage it ("as far as it depends on you").

Charles Spurgeon said that he loved all of God's people, but there were some of them that he wouldn't get along with 'til he got to Heaven.

Many people have misunderstood the last part of Romans 12:20— "You will heap burning coals on his head" (yeee-ouch!). Sounds like a scorching, but that would contradict everything in verses 19-21.

Barbara Bowen[11] provides Middle Eastern illumination for this "burning coals" phrase. The Bible-lands are countries where water jars, fruit baskets, etc., are carried on the head. If an ancient Middle Easterner's fire had gone out on her brazier, she might "run next door" to a neighbor to get help. The neighbor—in kindness—would place live coals in the brazier on the borrowing woman's head to carry home. In so doing, she would be "heap[ing] burning coals" on her neighbor's head. This would mean a blessing—not a burned scalp!

F. W. Boreham commented, "It occurred to me whilst we were playing that life itself is but a game of dominoes. Its highest art lies in matching your companion's pieces. The player who is left with empty hands wins everything. Victory lies in paying out the little ivory tablets with as prodigal a hand as possible. It is better in dominoes to give than to keep."[12]

10

CIVIL GOVERNMENT AND BEING CIVIL

Romans 13

The country—Hegemonia. Hegemonia has been sending colonists to the country of Euphoria. As more time lapses, the colonists from Hegemonia become increasingly incensed at the hegemons (or top leaders) of Hegemonia. The hegemons keep raising the taxes of the colonists of Euphoria, but the colonists feel they have little say with the hegemons.

The hegemons say the Bible supports them, because Romans 13:1 says that God ordained government and Romans 13:7 says that taxes are to support the government. But the Euphorians are fed up and secede from Hegemonia. Who is in the right?

Got it? Change the name of Hegemonia to England in 1770 and Euphoria to the United States-to-be, oversimplify, and you have what is called the American Revolution. If you were an Englander living in the 1770's, what would you think about such a bunch of political rebels? Neither evangelist John Wesley nor Bible commentator Matthew Henry approved of the American Revolution—on Biblical grounds as they saw them.

Patriotic Americans neatly overlook or reexplain the founding of their country when pounding their fists about Romans 13. What about it? Is Romans 13 as absolute as the Ten Commandments, or is it bendable?

Throughout church history Romans 13 has been looked upon as the classic statement of the Christian understanding of the role of government. As one modern church historian put it: "The thirteenth chapter of the Epistle to the Romans contains what are perhaps the most important words ever written for the history of political thought."[1] While Romans 13 is not the only New Testament set of pronouncements on human government, it contains the greatest concentration and perspective-provider on civil government that a New Testament writer offers. In Matthew 22:21 Jesus made the classic pronouncement upon the spheres of government and God. In Acts 4:19 and 5:29 Peter issued to governmental officials an exceptional case of civil disobedience. Paul also took to task on one occasion local officials who had violated his civil rights (Acts 16:37-39).

While there are certain exceptions to unquestioning obedience to governmental authority within the Bible, the overall guidelines for Christians with reference to government call for respect and cooperation. When Paul penned Romans 13, the Roman government, under Nero, had not yet begun its campaign of persecution against the Christians. The authorities had actually protected Paul against violence.[2] Yet, just a few years later, even after a number of imprisonments, Paul had not changed his mind (about the principles he had layed down in Romans 13) when he wrote Titus 3:1.[3]

Civil religion, politicians and prayer breakfasts, Watergate, pacificism, conscientious objectors, Christians and war, police brutality, voting, democracy, communism, dictatorships, pros and cons of capital punishment, taking out insurance policies, income tax—all of these issues make Romans 13:1-8 quite a soccer ball to kick around!

Government's Source and Force (Rom. 13:1-7)

Imagine that it is 1940 and you are a German citizen. Adolf Hitler has become the fuehrer. Romans 13:1 says that "there is no authority except that which God has established." John White wrote that "patriotism . . . led some [Plymouth] Brethren Assemblies [which is a conservative Christian group that takes the Bible very literally] to back Hitler's Nazi regime."[4] Other Protestants defied Hitler. For example, many Protestant professors were dismissed from university teaching posts by Hitler's soldiers.

As he reflected later on his own stance, Pastor Martin Niemoller said of Hitler's soldiers, "When they came for the Jews, I didn't speak up because I wasn't a Jew. When they came for the Communists, I didn't speak up because I wasn't a Communist. When they came for the Catholics, I didn't speak up because I wasn't a Catholic. When they came for me, there was nobody left to speak up." By contrast, Corrie ten Boom's family hid the Jewish people for Christ's sake.

How would you have handled such ticklish situations in Nazi Germany? Would you have demonstrated in Civil Rights marches? Do you think a Christian should have protested against the Viet Nam War as immoral? Do you think a British Christian should have stood against the American Revolution in the 1770's as wrong?

Herbert J. Philbrick, spy and counterspy, was once featured in the popular TV series, *I Led Three Lives*. In one sense every Christian leads more than one life—being a citizen of more than one kingdom.

 The apostle Paul lived under the totalitarian regime of the Caesars. "When he wrote [Romans 13] . . . Tiberius, Caligula, and Claudius had already been on the throne."[5] Since Nero was 12 years old in A.D. 50, Romans 13 was penned after Nero had begun to rule.[6]

Romans 13 has a logical tie-in with the preceding passage. In Romans 12:19 Paul ordered: "My dear friends, do not seek revenge, but leave a place for divine retribution" (NEB). Interestingly, Paul proceeded to comment that the Roman rulers were "God's agents of punishment, for retribution on the offender" (13:4, NEB). The same Greek word is used in Romans 12:19 and 13:4. The given individual can "leave room for God's wrath" (12:19, NIV) because the governmental institution is "an agent of wrath [the same Greek word as in 12:19] on the wrongdoer" (13:4).

Romans 13:1-7 is outlined below:

Obedience to government (vs. 1);

Opposition to government (vs. 2);

Objectives of government (vss. 3-5);

Obligations to government (vss. 6, 7).

 The kickoff statement in Romans 13:1 is: "Obey the government, for God is the one who has put it there" (LB). Some ancient writings have been found that credit the Roman emperor Julian (the Apostate) with taunting Christians with such a command. He said that they must "be patient, for this is the commandment of your God."[7]

SHOULD SUBJECTS ALWAYS "BE SUBJECT"?
Martin Luther's *Secular Authority: To What Extent It Should Be Obeyed?* (1523) "was the first and most definitive statement on the separation of church and state."[8] Luther said that "the prince is not to be obeyed if he requires service in a war manifestly unjust, as when Joachim of Brandenburg enlisted soldiers ostensibly against the Turk but really against the Lutherans."[9] Yet, Luther endorsed the death of thousands of Protestant peasants by civil rulers.

Church historian Bruce Shelley declared, "In the Netherlands . . . Calvinist ministers were among the earliest leaders of resistance groups. Today we would call them freedom fighters, or perhaps guerillas. The liberation leader of the national party in the northern province of the Netherlands was William the Silent." Again, Shelley wrote that John Knox of Scotland "developed the theory that Protestants had the right to resist, by force if necessary, any Roman Catholic ruler who tried to prevent their worship and mission." Bruce Shelley, *Church History in Plain Language*, pp. 280, 281).

? Were these early Protestants right or wrong? What are the goals of good government?

Ralph Martin[10] stated the overall objectives of civil government: "to promote good and to prevent evil." Civil government, then, should be aligned in its aims with the character of God (as expressed in the Book of Romans, namely, "the righteousness of God"; Rom. 1:17; 3:5, 26; 6:13, 18-20; 8:4). Whether at the individual level (chaps. 3—5) or the institutional level (chap. 13), God's goal is the production of righteousness.

? How would you evaluate the following statement: "When Paul expressed the view that rulers are not a terror to good conduct, he assumed that the authorities would reward the good and reprimand the wicked. This is an empirical rule. When the sword becomes a menace to the good, the whole purpose of government is subverted and, at that point, a revolution may be an ethical necessity, a Christian duty."[11]

J. B. Phillips rendered verse 3: "The honest citizen has no need to fear the keepers of law and order." The business of government is "law and order." Right should be the basis of law, while might (vs. 4) is a necessary support of order. Augustine said, "Without justice what are kingdoms but great gangs of robbers?"[12] This is what happens in a nation where might replaces right. Yet, as Alva McClain once said, "Law without penalty is just good advice."

For a Christian the compulsion to cooperate with civil government is not only because of "possible punishment" (vs. 5), but primarily "because of conscience" (vs. 5). Contrast with this motivation the assertion of writer Leo Tolstoy: "All the state obligations are against the conscience of a Christian: the oath of allegiance, taxes, law proceedings and military service." Leo Tolstoy, *Works*, XX, p. 275ff.). However, in line with Paul's general guideline, Ralph Martin claimed, "The moral constitution [or conscience] of the believer approves the moral constitution of the state."[13] While Paul Tillich had many misleading ideas in his theology, the following statement is one that the apostle Paul would undoubtedly approve: "If law is not internalized in conscience, then conscience must be externalized in law . . . . Laws are not passed to make bad people good, but innocent people safe."

To have officers in civil government functioning *for us* means financial obligations *by us*. "This is . . . why you pay taxes"—so civil servants can "give their full time to governing" (vs. 6). Not only personal taxes must be paid, but verse 7 mentions "revenue," probably referring to tax that is put on imports and exports. Along with financial obligations come "respect" and "honor" to authorities.

Our Most Taxing Tax (Rom. 13:8-10)

The Living Bible captures the essence of verse 8 in modern language: "Pay all your debts except the debt of love for others—never finish paying that!" (vs. 8). The bridge between Romans 13:1-7 and 13:8-10 is the word "owe" (vs. 8). The Good News Bible renders verse 6: "Pay, then, what you owe them." But does that duty discharge all our debt? No. Christians are charged: "Let no debt remain outstanding, except the continuing debt to love one another" (vs. 8). Christians owe a love-tax, and it is a never ending revenue payment to be made.

Two words—"love" and "law"—are found in both Romans 13:8 and 10. What is the relationship between "law" and "love"? In verse 9 Paul shifted from civil law (13:1-7) to moral Law (that is, the Ten Commandments). Paul parades forth the so-called second tablet of the Decalogue (Ex. 20:13-17).

Do not commit adultery,
Do not murder,
Do not steal,
Do not covet . . . (Rom. 13:9).

Next, as if to corral any strays that might conceivably have escaped the lariat, Paul added, "whatever other commandments there may be." The Living Bible captures verse 9, "All ten are wrapped up in this one, to love your neighbor as you love yourself." If the Law curbs and provides a guardrail (note the four "not's Paul tied together in vs. 9), love provides an engine that promotes positive care. The great church leader Augustine (c. A.D. 300), said, "Love, and do as you like." He was not flaunting the Law, but simply acknowledging what Paul affirmed in Romans 13:10—"love is the fulfillment of the law."

 In what ways is love like a tax?

It's 'High Time' (Rom. 13:11-14)

Have you ever heard someone talk about having a "high old time"? They usually have in mind anything but what Paul has in mind when he says that "it is high time to awake out of sleep" (13:11, KJV). A moral alarm clock had just gone off. When Paul wrote that "the day is almost here," (vs. 12), it was a "vivid picture for day-break."[14] As if we were tossing aside our pajamas, Christians are to "put aside the deeds of darkness" (Rom. 13:12). We are to don "the armor of light."

The "let us" of verse 12 is followed by the "let us" of verse 13. A "high time" for a Christian is quite the opposite pole from a "high old time" of a non-Christian. Paul outlaws three pairs of activities or attitudes: "wild parties and getting drunk or . . . adultery and lust, or fighting, or jealousy" (vs. 13, LB).

The last verse urges us to make no pre-plans for sin. Indeed, take contraceptive measures toward sin. Stocking shelves with cookies means planning to break diets. Planning not to have a private pity-party means planning positively by calling a friend to arrange a wholesome activity together. No fodder and no flame means no fire!

CHAPTER
11
DOES WHAT'S MATERIAL MATTER?
ROMANS 14:1—15:7

A young woman went to Venezuela as a short-term missionary. While she was serving Christ there, she thought it would be a dandy idea to organize the children at Vacation Bible School into baseball teams. Since they were short on equipment, arms served as bats and lemons as balls.

The children appeared to be having fun, but the mission leader felt it necessary to put a halt to the baseball games. He explained to the short-termer that for many Christians in Venezuela baseball is a no-no. The reason for this is that Venezuelans bet money on baseball games there in the way Americans do on race horses. Consequently, as a form of testimony to non-Christian Venezuelans, the Christians there generally refrain from playing baseball—probably in the same way many American Christians might turn down the opportunity of spending time at a racetrack here.[1] Most Christians in America would have little conscience about attending a baseball game or watching one on TV. In Venezuela, however, that is a touchy question. How should a Christian handle touchy issues like this?

A companion passage to Romans 14:1—15:7 is I Corinthians 8—10. Because they overlap in subject matter and were probably written within the same general time belt (likely within A.D. 54-57), I Corinthians 8—10 should be considered here for the light it might throw onto Romans 14. Read the two together.

Among the series of hot topics (see I Cor. 5:1; 7:1; 8:1; 12:1) Paul addressed to Corinthian Christians, one revolved "about food

93

sacrificed to idols" (I Cor. 8:1). The local pagan temple at Corinth had something like a cut-rate meat market next door to it, where the best bargains on beefsteak in town could be bought.

Realizing that "an idol is nothing at all" (I Cor. 8:4), some Christians refused to view bargain steaks as if they had sin germs crawling on them. "Let's eat" was their view. Other sensitive-minded Christians "with a weak conscience" (8:10)—probably from a Jewish background—were horrified that Christians should be contaminated by anything associated with idolatry. Paul didn't want new believers from pagan backgrounds to trip up and "fall into sin" (8:13).

Commentator John Knox[2] observed certain parallel subjects treated in Romans and I Corinthians.

Spiritual gifts	Romans 12:4-8	I Cor. 12 and 14
Love	Romans 13:8-10	I Cor. 13
"Strong" and "weak" Christians	Romans 14	I Cor. 8—10

A Polarizing Church (Rom. 14:1-4)

Two groups in the early Roman Christian church were in danger of becoming polarized—the "weak" (14:1, 2) and the "strong" (15:1).

One of the difficulties of our text lies in transferring the terms "weak" (14:1) and "strong" (15:1) into modern meanings. "Conservative" and "liberal" do not provide equivalents if we are thinking about theology. Furthermore, we cannot make the "weak" equal to what modern Christians sometimes call "legalists." A legalist only scolds others for not coming up to what he or she thinks are correct standards, but the legalist is in no danger (like "the weak" Christian of Rom. 14) of being drawn down into some sin by the "strong." Neither is the "strong" Christian simply an indifferent one.

"The 'weak' brother can be defined as one whose conscience works in overdrive, but like a car spinning its wheels on ice, it doesn't get him anywhere. He makes issues out of . . . things of no essential importance, attaching to them a moral character they do not possess."[3] Basically, the issue revolves around Romans 14:14. The "strong" Christian is the one who understands that material things in our world are amoral (that is, not inherently sinful). For instance, he recognizes "that an idol stands for something that does not really exist" (I Cor. 8:4, GNB). Steaks sacrificed to statues have just as many vitamins as those dedicated to idols, and are equally edible.

By contrast, the "weak" Christian has hang-ups about eating food connected with idol worship. He was probably once all tangled up in the sin of idol worship, so he can't get it through his head that meat is just meat—whether it comes from a Satanist temple or from Ralph's Pretty Good Grocery. Similarly, when 200 people were polled as to why they didn't return to a conservative church meeting in a mall, 50 replied that it was because the church met in a movie theater.

In the Roman churches, questions of diet (14:2, 3) and days (14:4, 5) became hot-potato issues. Paul counseled the strong Christians: "Welcome [one] whose faith is weak, but not with the idea of arguing over his scruples" (14:1, J. B. Phillips). Paul recognized in these verses that disagreements would exist among Christians. They must agree to disagree without being unduly disagreeable.

A TRUE CONFESSION

The fact is that no Christian really wants to be called or considered "weak." However, we may be "weak" at one time and not at another. Or we may be "weak" on one issue and not others.

This writer confesses that he is "weak" concerning TV. I have not owned a television during my adult life. I readily admit that there is nothing inherently sinful about a TV. In fact, I usually go to a friend's home who owns a TV if there is some valuable classic to watch. Furthermore, I have no hesitation about going to a worthwhile movie. Consequently, I am acknowledging that there is nothing intrinsically sinful about TVs. However, I know myself well enough to know that if I did own one, it would be catering to my own sinful habits—of over-indulging and of watching shows that are unquestionably harmful to me. As a result, I declare myself a "weak" Christian (in the Pauline sense of the word) on that particular item—television watching. In other areas, I view myself as "strong" and would not be greatly bothered about some activities or things that might bother some other Christians.

Paul Little[4] asked, "So what do we do about weak brothers? Bowl them over and keep rolling? Some of the Roman Christians must have felt like saying, 'Phooey on weak brothers anyway! They're just immature, so why bother?' " By contrast, Paul urged the strong to welcome the weak (Rom. 14:1), "but not to doubtful disputations" (KJV). This last phrase is a difficult one to understand. The Good News Bible renders it: "Do not argue with him about his personal opinions." William Barclay suggested this possible meaning: "Do not introduce him straight away to the discussion of questions which can only raise doubts."[5] (The term "faith" in verse 1 evidently means one's "beliefs" or "convictions.")

As a specific sample of the two types of Christian's convictions, Paul mentioned vegetarians and meat eaters (14:2, 3). Whatever the particular issue, Paul pleads for understanding. James Engel illustrated (what Paul *didn't* want) with a conversation between two Christians touring a factory. One Christian was heard to say, "You know, that assembly line is pretty much like my church. We produce just one standard model, and those that don't fit the mold are treated as rejects and sent back for further work."[6] But God is able to take both (and all) kinds of Christians into the fellowship of the Church.

In verse 3 Paul addressed both types of Christians (first the strong, then the weak). Paul Little illustrated the apostle's advice as follows: "Let's apply it to a noncontroversial activity like putting together jig-saw puzzles. I may feel that I have the liberty to work on a puzzle. This liberty does not give me the right to call the person who refrains an 'old fogey.' On the other hand, perhaps I don't [feel I] have the liberty to indulge in this pastime. I can't consequently accuse another Christian of being worldly because he sits down with a puzzle."[7] All Christians need to realize, then, that other solid Christians sincerely seeking to serve the Lord may have varying views from their own on many matters not central to the core of Christianity.

Judged, Not Judgmental (Rom. 14:5-12)

Imagine two Jews who have become Christians meeting on the street in A.D. 35. One says, "I'm glad I'm a Christian now and worship on the first day of the week. All those Saturday rules were killing me." The other Jew appears visibly upset. "What do you mean? The Sabbath is an integral part of our sacred heritage. Just because we're Christians doesn't mean I'm any less Jewish. I value that day!"

Many Christians can only appreciate the second Jew's problem if they were suddenly asked to worship on Tuesday rather than on Sunday. Ingrained tradition would shout at them: "Sunday's the right day. How dare you?"

Now imagine having to referee between two such viewpoints, and you get some inkling into Paul's predicament. He had to be "Dear Abby" over disputes about days and diets (14:5, 6). Paul instructed: "Let every one be definite in his own convictions [on those subjects]" (14:5b, J. B. Phillips). Each Christian must arrive at his or her own judgment on many matters unsettled by Scripture. No need for judgmentalness (14:10), for "we shall all be judged one day . . . by the judgment of God" (14:11, J. B. Phillips).

UPDATING DAYS

Before Fred became a Christian, he was a golf fiend. He virtually worshiped golf. He ate, drank, and slept golf balls. Through a friend, Christ entered Fred's life at the Vermont Avenue Church. George, a longtime Christian, tried to take Fred under his wing, show him friendship and help Fred grow. However, George's job required him to work six days a week at a desk job. A medical doctor recommended strongly that George take up some physical exercise, so he decided to play golf Sunday afternoons (his one day off).

One day George invited Fred to join him for golf. He found Fred horrified. Why, just that week Fred had heard a radio preacher say that people idolized night clubs by night and golf clubs by day. Fred acted appalled, "How can you do such a thing as a Christian?" he asked George. "And on the Lord's Day at that!"

? How would you advise Fred and George in light of Romans 14 and I Corinthians 8—10?

When Right Can Be Wrong (Rom. 14:13-23)

Here's the drift of these eleven verses:[8]
  Don't judge (vs. 13)—to the weak;
  Don't grieve (vs. 15)—to the strong;
  Don't destroy (vs. 20)—to both groups.

Ω F. F. Bruce commented on the two uses of "judge" in verse 13: "In the former clause 'judge' means 'criticize'; in the latter it means 'decide.' In Greek, as in English, the same word . . . does duty for both senses."[9] The New English Bible captures the word play in verse 13: "Let us therefore cease judging one another, but rather make this simple judgement: that no obstacle or stumbling-block be placed in a brother's way."

What's the matter with matter (that is, the material world)? The Christian view (as opposed to false spiritualist views) is that nothing's automatically the matter with matter. As evangelist Leighton Ford pointed out, the opposite of spiritual (in the Christian sense) is not material, but sin. Paul was persuaded (14:14): "there is nothing unclean of itself [or intrinsically evil]" (KJV).

Matter (that is, grass, trees, pool tables, communion tables, Ping Pong balls, chalices, vases, tobacco, buttercups, TV screens, the human anatomy, etc.) is very real, but it should not matter most for a Christian (II Cor. 4:18). Nor are material items sinful in and of themselves. This is the paramount principle enunciated by Paul in Romans 14:14. Meat offered to idols did not crawl with sin germs.

There is no significant material difference between a gambling table and a communion table in their physical makeup, although there is in their use.

The view that there is something the matter with matter (that is, things in our physical world) is a sub-Christian view. C. S. Lewis said, "God loves material things—He made them." Often Christians have fallen prey to this error and paraded false spiritual views as being Christian.

Even though Paul was talking about what was right, "if someone believes it is wrong, then he shouldn't do it because for him it is wrong" (14:14, LB). Thus, what was right for Paul could be mentally wrong for another Christian. (We are not talking here about absolutes like the Ten Commandments.)

The terms "distressed" in verse 15 and "offended" (KJV) in verse 21 are often misunderstood, because they are used by Paul in a different way than we use those terms today. Today, to be "grieved," or "offended" means to be upset (as "feels pained" sounds in The Berkeley Version; 14:15). However, Paul has in mind far more than being emotionally upset.

For instance, if some believer should come up to you and say, "That purple shirt offends me as a Christian," he would not be using the word "offends" (KJV) as Paul does. To "offend" in Paul's use of the word would mean that the offended would be tempted to go out and follow his obsession to buy purple shirts, which would go against his conscience. In other words, an "offended" person (in Paul's use) ends up in sin ("cause . . . to fall," 14:21, NIV) because of your perfectly permissible action.

Missionary Tom Watson said, "If you considered everyone's objections and used I Corinthians 8 and Romans 14 [wrongly], you'd have to dress in a straitjacket and cut your hair like Yul Brynner."

In other words, Paul does not mean that we have to stop doing what someone objects to because they say it "offends" them. He is talking about tripping up less informed believers so they stumble back into sin.

Since what matters most to God are matters like peace, "let us therefore follow after . . . peace" (vs. 19). Don't create a stew over some stewmeat (vs. 20)! What is material becomes quite immaterial (that is, irrelevant) in light of the larger issues at stake.

BETTER NOT TO BUTT

Alexander Whyte quoted Martin Luther as saying: "If two goats meet each other in a narrow path above a piece of water, what do they do? They cannot turn back, and they cannot pass each other, and there is not an inch of spare room. If they were to butt each other, both would fall into the water below and be drowned. What will they do, do you suppose?"

"Well, nature has taught the one goat to lie down and let the other pass over it, and then they both get to the end of the way safe and sound."

The moral: better not to butt heads with your brothers and sisters whose convictions differ from yours.

He Is Heavy, but He's My Brother (Rom. 15:1-7)

The country song is quite Christian in its lyrics at this point:

> Help me be a little meeker
> With the brother that is weaker,

> Think a little more of others,
> And a little less of me.

The famous Boys' Town motto was: "He's not heavy; he's my brother." Indeed, sometimes that other Christian may feel more like a *bother* than a brother.

But we have the example of Christ the Burden Bearer (15:3). In short, the Golden Rule applies at a higher level. We must treat one another the way Christ has treated us (15:7).

12

SIGNING OFF
ROMANS 15:8—16:27

Racial Integration (Rom. 15:8-21)

Face, race, place, space, grace—all of us bring our own ideas about those things to church. Each comes with his or her own ethnic identity and ethical ideals. The church is the life laboratory for overcoming our racism, sexism, classism, etc.

Based on archaeological and historical research findings, scholars can get a good estimate of population trends in the ancient world. Ralph Martin notes that "no fewer than thirteen synagogues in Rome ministered to a Jewish population of between forty and fifty thousand (out of a total population between 700,000 and one million)."[1]

The word "Jews" in 15:8 and "Gentiles" found eight times in 15:9-21 alerts us to the interplay between these two groups—which brought on some powder-keg issues. Paul summoned Scriptural support—

II Samuel 22:50; Psalm 18:49—in Romans 15:9;
Deuteronomy 32:43—in 15:10;
Psalm 117:1—in 15:11;
Isaiah 11:10—in 15:12.

Thus, we see forecasted the integration of Jews "among the Gentiles" (15:9). The Gentiles are "with his people," the Jews (15:10). Each would be bringing mental baggage to unload. They would need "hope . . . joy and peace" to work together harmoniously (15:13).

OPPOSITE OUTLOOKS
"Gentlemen, the situation in the church is hopeless, and nothing can

be done" intoned the church chairman at the business meeting right after he stopped praying to "Almighty God."

By contrast, Winston Churchill, faced with the stark condition that Britain found itself in toward the end of World War II, told his dispirited cabinet, "Gentlemen, I find it rather inspiring."[2]

Twixt' optimist and pessimist
The difference is droll.
The optimist sees the doughnut;
The pessimist sees the hole.
—source unknown
(P.S. Does the faith-realist see the whole?)

Paul's "priestly duty" was "to be a minister . . . to the Gentiles" (15:16).

? Do you ever think of yourself as a "priest"? How do you exercise your priesthood?

As part of "proclaiming the gospel of God" (15:16), Paul "fully proclaimed the gospel of Christ" (15:19). Illyricum (or Dalmatia) was the region northwest from Macedonia on the coast of the Adriatic Sea between modern Greece and Italy. However, no account of these adventures is available from Acts. Paul's magnificent obsession was "to preach the gospel" (15:20) in virgin territory.

Like the title line from the Star Trek TV series, Paul wanted "to boldly go where no man has gone before." When David Livingstone volunteered as a missionary with the London Missionary Society, they asked him where he would like to go. "Anywhere," he said, "so long as it is forward."[3]

Triptick Alterations (Rom. 15:22-29)

Politicians often have to explain policy changes to voters. Likewise, Paul had to explain himself concerning, (1) his postponement of his trip to Rome (15:22-24), and (2) his plan for a trip to Jerusalem

(15:25-29). Also, Spain had become Paul's "new Macedonia." Did Paul ever embark upon this fourth missionary trip to Spain? History remains mute.

While silence enshrouds Paul's Spanish destination, the Biblical record supplies data concerning a collection carried to Jerusalem (Acts 19:21; 20:4; I Cor. 16:1; II Cor. 8 and 9).

Co-Strugglers (Rom. 15:30-33)

Paul not only planned "coming to you [Romans]" (15:22), but he proposed that they pray that I, Paul, "may come to you" (15:32). The Romans could enter Paul's "struggle by praying" (15:30).

Christian Hellos (Rom. 16:1-24)

Ralph Martin wrote, "As Hebrews 11 has been termed the 'picture gallery' of Old Testament saints, so we may call Romans 16 the 'picture gallery' of New Testament believers."[4] It seems strange to us that Paul penned his two longest lists of named greetings to churches he had evidently never visited—twenty-six are greeted by name in Romans (16) and eight in the to-and-from greetings of Colossians (4:10-17; cf. 2:1). In churches where Paul was known, he probably did not want to risk people getting their feelings hurt by possible omissions. Long lists of greetings like this were virtually unknown before Paul's day.[5]

❝ The critic Renan said of Phoebe: "She bore in the folds of her robe the whole future of Christian theology" (as letter carrier of the Romans epistle).　　—in Edmond Hiebert, *Personalities Around Paul*, p. 196

Cordially commended to Christians at Rome was Phoebe (*FEE-bee*), whose name (meaning "bright" or "radiant") is found only here in the New Testament. She is the only one called by Paul "our sister."

? Who is a Phoebe (i.e., radiant) Christian you have known?

Phoebe is labeled a "servant." The idea of "servant" may have technical (*diakonos, or* "deacon") or nontechnical nuances (i.e., a helper).

 "In his famous letter to the Emperor Trajan, Pliny speaks of examining Christians in Bithynia, among whom were 'two slave women called ministers.' "[6] Arguing for the technical usage of *diakonos* (dee-AH-kone-ahs), Alvera and Berkeley Mickelsen pointed out: *"Living Letters* [a modern paraphrase Bible translation] does the gravest injustice to

103

Phoebe. In reference to Timothy, it translates *diakonos* as 'pastor' (I Tim. 4:6). But of Phoebe in Romans 16:1, *Living Letters* says, 'a dear Christian woman . . . .' "[7]

? Do you think women should be ministers? What role do you think women play or should play in the life of a local church?

Phoebe was certified by the church at Cenchrea (16:1), the port city for Corinth in Achaia.

Ω The Greek term behind "a great help" (16:2) occurs only here in the New Testament. Edmond Hiebert noted that in other contexts the word had the connotations of "protectress, patroness, or guardian."[8] The *Westminster Bible Dictionary* thinks that the "term may imply that she made it a duty to stand by foreigners in their civic helplessness" (p. 750).

? Have you known any church or individual who has sponsored refugees? How did they help these people?

Tents move a lot. And so did Priscilla and Aquila (which does not rhyme with Priscilla, but is pronounced *ACK-wih-luh*), tentmakers. In the New Testament annals this mobile couple lived in Corinth (Acts 18:1-3), Ephesus (Acts 18:19), Rome (Rom. 16:3), and once more at Ephesus (II Tim. 4:19). The Emperor Claudius had expelled Jews from Rome in A.D. 49. This cordial, capable couple had a profound impact upon Paul and Apollos (Acts 18:24-28). On four of the six occasions where this team of two are mentioned, Priscilla's name is mentioned first. Like Epaphroditus in Philippians 2:30, this husband-wife duo were riskers (Rom. 16:4). They co-hosted a house church in Rome (16:5; cp. Philem. 2).

The mobility of those times is again seen in Epenetus (*e-PEE-ne-tus*) at Rome, who had been "the first convert to Christ in the province of Asia" (16:5). Epenetus was over 800 miles from his spiritual maternity ward.

Ω Mary (16:6) is one of possibly ten women mentioned in Romans 16:1-16. There is some debate about the gender of the second individual in 16:7. Bible translations that have Junias (NIV) understand the person to be masculine; those with Junia (KJV) assume the character to be feminine. One reason some translators select the masculine is that if we allow the feminine gender in 16:7, then we must grant that this may be a reference to a woman apostle. Bruce Metzger stated of *Junia:* "It's a proper name in the accusative [case], so you can't tell whether it's masculine or feminine, but almost all instances in antiquity are feminine. If we go on a percentage basis, the feminine is more likely"[9]

The couple (whether two men, or male and female) are:

(1) "outstanding among the apostles" (if they are part of the apostles in its broader meaning; see Acts 14:4, 14 which includes Barnabas); or

(2) "respected in the circle of the apostles" (hence, outside the apostles' circle but respected by those inside it).

Still a third translation problem is that Andronicus and Junia(s) may be understood as:

(1) physical "relatives" of Paul (NIV); or

(2) "kinsmen" (KJV), i.e., fellow Jews.

? Who would you include on your own list of Christians you would greet with complimentary characteristics (such as in 16:8-12)?

Probably Rufus (in 16:13) was the son of Simon of Cyrene (Mk. 15:21), since strong tradition indicates Mark's Gospel was written to Rome (cf. I Pet. 5:13 where Mark is mentioned and "Babylon" is most probably a secret code word for Rome).

After the lengthiest list in the New Testament Epistles of the named faithful, Paul alluded to some unnamed unfaithful ones (16:17-19). "Watch out . . . keep away" (16:17), Paul must warn against their winsome words. Paul is rough on "smooth talk"ers (16:18).

Two classic Pauline terms—"peace" and "grace" (16:19)—grace the conclusion of Paul's letter. Yet Leon Morris noted, "Nothing could more graphically illustrate the fact that peace in the New Testament is not simply the absence of war" as to describe the "God of peace" (16:19) as engaged in the warlike activity of "crush[ing] Satan."[10]

Four friends of Paul passed on greetings in 16:21. Tertius the stenographer (16:22) is found only here in the New Testament, although Paul obviously used secretaries on other occasions. Three other Gaiuses (16:23) are mentioned in the New Testament (Acts 19:29; 20:4; I Cor. 1:14), but Gaius was the equivalent of John Doe in ancient Roman lawbooks—a common name.

Ω "An inscription discovered in Corinth and dating from the first century reads: 'Erastus, the commissioner of public works, laid this pavement at his own expense.' Strictly, 'commissioner of public works' is not the same as 'city treasurer'; but it is natural to think either that Erastus [Rom. 16:23] advanced from commissioner to treasurer or that he was demoted from treasurer to commissioner."[11]

A Geyser of Adoration (Rom. 16:25-27)

The last three verses of Romans irrupt in a geyser of praise "to him who is able . . . to the only wise God" (16:25, 27).

"On October 2, 1925, at St. Leonard's-on-Sea, Sussex, John Logie Baird, after having spent long, lean years in seemingly unproductive research in a garret, dashed madly downstairs and grabbing the first person he met, dragged him up to his room, set him down unceremoniously in front of his lamps and cameras and gave him, unknown to the lad himself, the honor of being the first person ever to appear on television! Yes, it must be an intoxicating experience to make a great scientific discovery."[12]

Strictly speaking, the Gospel (16:25) is not a discovery, but a divine disclosure; not merely a human revolution, but a divine revelation (16:25, 26). Paul closes, as it were, by putting his patent on "my gospel" (16:25). Is it your Gospel, too—lock, stock, and barrel?

Notice that the commencement and conclusion of Romans overlap—one characteristic feature of good writing.

ROMANS 1	ROMANS 16
"the gospel" (vss. 1, 2)	"my gospel" (vs. 25)
God "promised beforehand" (vs. 2)	"hidden for long ages past" (vs. 25)
"through his prophets in in the Holy Scriptures" (vs. 2)	"through the prophetic writings" (vs. 26)
"all the Gentiles" (vs. 5)	"all nations" (vs. 26)
"obedience that comes from faith" (vs. 5)	"might believe and obey" (vs. 26)
"to Jesus Christ" (vs. 6)	"through Jesus Christ" (vs. 27)

> "Paul began his book by referring to a gospel that had always been known; and he closes by referring to a mystery that had never been known."　　　　—Alva McClain, *Romans: The Gospel of God's Grace*

Thus, Paul is justified in holding to his Gospel (16:25), God is justified in his dealings with Israel (chaps. 9—11), and any sinner can be justified by believing in the God who justifies the ungodly through faith in Jesus (4:5). That is the jugular vein of the Book of Romans.

NOTES

Chapter 1

[1] Louis Berkhof, *Systematic Theology* (Grand Rapids: Eerdmans, 1941), p. 511.

[2] J. Agar Beet, *A Commentary on St. Paul's Epistle to the Romans* (London: Hodder and Stoughton, 1902), p. 38.

[3] Alva McClain, *Romans: The Gospel of God's Grace* (Chicago: Moody Press, 1973), p. 45.

[4] In Wilbur Smith, *Therefore Stand* (Boston: W. A. Wilde Co., 1945), p. 31.

[5] Michael Green, *Evangelism in the Early Church* (Grand Rapids: Eerdmans, 1970), p. 78.

[6] *Bibliotheca Sacra.*

[7] In Augustus Strong, *Systematic Theology* (Westwood, NJ: Revell, 1907), p. 27.

[8] *Our Daily Bread.*

[9] Will Durant, *Oriental Heritage* (New York: Simon and Schuster, 1935), p. 5.

[10] Ray Stedman, *From Guilt to Glory, I* (Portland, OR: Multnomah Press, 1986), p. 25.

[11] Donald Grey Barnhouse, *Man's Ruin* (Wheaton, IL: Van Kampen Press, 1953), p. 287.

[12] Berkeley Mickelsen, in *Wycliffe Bible Commentary*, eds. Charles Pfeiffer and Everett Harrison (Chicago: Moody Press, 1962), p. 1187.

Chapter 2

[1] *Christianity Today*, 9 April, 1976.

[2] Source unknown.

[3] Source unknown.

[4] Alexander Maclaren, *Expositions of Holy Scripture, XXXII* (London: A. C. Armstrong and Son, 1908), p. 200

[5] F. F. Bruce, *Commentary on the Epistles to the Ephesians and Colossians* (Grand Rapids: Eerdmans, 1957), p. 295.

[6] Ralph Martin, in *The New Bible Commentary: Revised* (Grand Rapids: Eerdmans, 1970), p. 1019.

[7] Steven Barabas, in *The Zondervan Pictorial Bible Dictionary*, ed. Merrill Tenney (Grand Rapids: Zondervan, 1963), pp. 180, 181.

[8] As outlined by Ralph Martin in *The New Bible Commentary: Revised* (Grand Rapids: Eerdmans, 1970), p. 1019.

[9] Mickelsen, *Wycliffe Bible Commentary*, p. 1189.

[10] Ernst Kasemann, *Commentary on Romans* (Grand Rapids: Eerdmans, 1978), p. 69.

[11] Martin, *New Bible Commentary: Revised*, p. 1019.

[12] E. H. Gifford, *The Epistle of St. Paul to the Romans* (London: John Murray, 1886).

[13] *William Barclay: A Spiritual Autobiography* (Grand Rapids: Eerdmans, 1977), p. 34.

Chapter 3

[1] Barnhouse, *Man's Ruin*, p. 2.

[2] Charles Ryrie, *A Survey of Bible Doctrine* (Chicago: Moody Press, 1972), p. 111.

[3] McClain, *Romans*, p. 91.

[4] Ibid., p. 101.

[5] Barnhouse, *God's Wrath* (Wheaton, IL: Van Kampen Press), p. 9.

[6] Lorman Petersen, *The Zondervan Pictorial Encyclopedia of the Bible, III* (Grand Rapids: Zondervan, 1975), p. 764.

[7] James Sanders, *Interpretation*, April, 1982, p. 155.

[8] John Murray, *Epistle to the Romans, I* (Grand Rapids: Eerdmans, 1959), p. 123.

[9] Martin Luther, in *Eerdmans Handbook to the History of Christianity* (Grand Rapids: Eerdmans, 1977), p. 360.

[10] Petersen, *Zondervan Pictorial Encyclopedia*, III, 768.
[11] H. C. Leupold, *Exposition of Genesis*, I (Grand Rapids: Baker, 1942), p. 476.
[12] M. E. Osterhaven, *Zondervan Pictorial Encyclopedia*, III, 265.
[13] A. T. Robertson, *Word Pictures of the New Testament*, IV (Nashville: Broadman Press, 1931), p. 350.
[14] E. D. Burton, *Galatians: International Critical Commentary* (Edinburgh: T and T Clark, 1921), p. 447.
[15] James Denney, in A. T. Robertson's *Word Pictures of the New Testament*, IV, 350.
[16] Quoted from Louis Berkhof, *Systematic Theology*, p. 512.
[17] F. F. Bruce, *Zondervan Pictorial Encyclopedia* V, 155.

Chapter 4
[1] Outline from Anders Nygren, *Commentary on Romans* (Philadelphia: Muhlenberg Press, 1949), p. 32
[2] James Moulton, *Prolegomena*, I (Edinburgh: T and T Clark, 1908), p. 110.
[3] A. Skevington Wood, *Life by the Spirit* (Grand Rapids: Zondervan, 1963), p. 74.
[4] F. Godet, *Commentary on St. Paul's Epistle to the Romans* (Grand Rapids: Zondervan, n.d.), p. 317.
[5] William Barclay, *A New Testament Wordbook* (New York: Harper and Row, 1958), p. 106.
[6] Ibid., pp. 106, 107.
[7] Ibid., p. 107.
[8] Stedman, *From Guilt to Glory*, I, 105.
[9] Ibid.
[10] K. E. Kirk, *Romans* (Oxford: Clarendon Press, 1937), p. 193.
[11] Stedman, *From Guilt to Glory*, I, 242.
[12] Cheryl Lavin, *Chicago Tribune Magazine*, 12 February, 1984.
[13] "The Day of Discovery," 5 July, 1970.
[14] C. S. Lewis, *The Problem of Pain* (New York: MacMillan, 1978), p. 91.
[15] George Eldon Ladd, *A Theology of the New Testament* (Grand Rapids: Eerdmans, 1974), p. 456.
[16] Charles Hodge, *Commentary on the Epistle to the Romans*.
[17] C. K. Barrett, *A Commentary on the Epistle to the Romans* (New York: Harper and Row, 1957), p. 108.
[18] Wrote Barclay, *More New Testament Words*, p. 103.
[19] Nygren, *Commentary on Romans*, p.207.
[20] Martin, *The New Bible Commentary: Revised*, p. 1026.
[21] In Geoffrey Bromiley, *Historical Theology: An Introduction* (Grand Rapids: Eerdmans, 1978), p. 23.

Chapter 5
[1] Steven Barabas, in *Zondervan Pictorial Bible Dictionary*, p. 751.
[2] Adam Clarke, *Christian Theology* (Salem, OH: The Convention Boodstore, 1967), p. 366.
[3] John Murray, in *Basic Christian Doctrines* (New York: Holt, Rinehart, and Winston, 1962), p. 232.
[4] Nygren, *Commentary on Romans*, p. 296.
[5] McClain, *Romans*, p. 28.
[6] Martin, *The New Bible Commentary: Revised*, p. 1014.
[7] In Eugene Nida, *Religion Across Cultures* (Pasadena, CA: William Carey Library, 1979), p. 18.
[8] Bruce, *Romans*, p. 134.
[9] F. F. Bruce, *The Zondervan Pictorial Encyclopedia of the Bible*, V, 156.
[10] Murray, *Romans*, I, 213.
[11] Strong, *Systematic Theology*, p. 941.
[12] J. Armitage Robinson, *The Body* (London: S. C. M. Press, 1957), p. 31.

[13] John Phillips, *Exploring Romans* (Chicago; Moody Press, 1971), pp. 106, 107.
[14] Barrett, *Romans*, p. 128.
[15] In *A General Introduction to Psychoanalysis* (Liveright, 1977).
[16] Stedman, *From Guilt to Glory*, I, 157.
[17] From *Our Daily Bread*
[18] Arnold Toynbee, *The Study of History* (New York: Oxford, 1947-57).

Chapter 6
[1] Nygren, *Romans*, p. 279.
[2] Leslie Allen, in Howley, Bruce, and Ellison, eds., *A New Testament Commentary* (Grand Rapids: Zondervan, 1969), p. 355.
[3] Murray, *Romans*, I, 229.
[4] Philip McNair, in *Eerdman's Handbook on the History of Christianity*, p. 353.
[5] George Turner, *Zondervan Pictorial Encyclopedia*, V, 267.
[6] According to Robert Jewett, *Interpretation*, January, 1980.
[7] McClain, *Romans*, p. 151.
[8] In Augustus Strong, *Systematic Theology*, p. 111.
[9] In Ralph Martin, *New Bible Commentary: Revised*, p. 1029.
[10] Stedman, *From Guilt to Glory*, I, 190.
[11] Keith Miller, *A Taste of New Wine* (Waco, TX: Word, 1966), p. 38.
[12] Illustration from Cornelius Jaarsma, *Human Development, Learning, and Teaching* (Grand Rapids: Eerdmans, 1961), p. 70.
[13] James Denney, in Ralph Martin, *The New Bible Commentary: Revised*, p. 1029.
[14] In R. G. Lee, *The Must of the Second Birth* (Westwood, NJ: Revell, 1959), p. 119.
[15] In Ernest Rattenbury's *The Evangelical Doctrines of Charles Wesley's Hymns* (London: Epworth Press, 1941), p. 124.

Chapter 7
[1] Bruce, *Romans*, p. 159.
[2] From T. W. Manson, in Matthew Black's *Romans* (Grand Rapids: Eerdmans, 1981), p. 114.
[3] Wood, *Life by the Spirit*, p. 20.
[4] Stuart Briscoe, *Romans: Communicator's Commentary* (Waco, TX: Word, 1987), pp. 153, 154.
[5] Godet, *Commentary on St. Paul's Epistle to the Romans*.
[6] Godet, *Romans*, p. 305.
[7] Wood, *Life by the Spirit*, p. 48.
[8] Donald Grey Barnhouse, *The Cross Through the Open Tomb*, p. 133.
[9] W. E. Vine, *Romans* (Grand Rapids: Zondervan, 1948), p. 117.
[10] In Ray Stedman, *From Guilt to Glory*, I, p. 229.
[11] As C. H. Dodd rendered Romans 8:22 in Matthew Black, *Romans*, p. 122.
[12] Godet, *Romans*, p. 316.
[13] Bruce, *Romans*, p. 173.
[14] From Griffith Thomas, *St. Paul's Epistle to the Romans* (Grand Rapids: Eerdmans, 1946), pp. 98, 99.
[15] From Stuart Babbage, *The Vacuum of Unbelief* (Grand Rapids: Zondervan, 1969), pp. 39, 40.
[16] Quoted in Philip Hughes's *Commentary on the Epistle to the Hebrews* (Grand Rapids: Eerdmans, 1977), p. 516.
[17] Donald Barnhouse, *Romans: God's Heirs* (Wheaton, IL: Van Kampen Press, 1953).
[18] Phillips, *Exploring Romans*.

Chapter 8
[1] F. W. Beare, *The Interpreter's Dictionary of the Bible*, IV (Nashville: Abingdon Press, 1962), p. 115.

[2] In Barnhouse, *Man's Ruin*, I, 177.
[3] Weiss, in B. B. Warfield, *The Person and Work of Christ* (Philadelphia: Presbyterian and Reformed Publishing Co., 1950), pp. 219, 220.
[4] Richard Longnecker, *Zondervan Pictorial Encyclopedia*, IV, 661.
[5] In Bromiley, ed., *Historical Theology: An Introduction*, p. 142.
[6] Martin, *The New Bible Commentary: Revised*, p. 1035.
[7] McClain, *Romans*, p. 183.
[8] Ibid., p. 188
[9] Everett Harrison, in *The Expositor's Bible Commentary*, X (Grand Rapids: Zondervan, 1976), p. 113.
[10] Quote from *The Speaker's Bible: Romans* (London: John Murray, 1886), p. 214.
[11] Kasemann, *Romans*, p. 293.
[12] Barclay, *Romans*, p. 141.
[13] D. P. Thomson in *The Speaker's Bible: Romans*, I, 217
[14] Barker, Lane, and Michaels, *The New Testament Speaks* (New York: Harper and Row, 1969), pp. 198, 201.
[15] Ralph Martin, in *The New Bible Commentary: Revised*, p. 1037.
[16] Bruce, *Romans*, p. 215.
[17] William Hendriksen, *Survey of the Bible* (Grand Rapids: Baker, 1947), p. 344.
[18] E. M. Blaiklock, *Commentary on the New Testament* (Old Tappan, NJ: Revell, 1977), p. 137.
[19] Bruce, *Romans*, p. 221.
[20] Ethelbert Stauffer, in Leslie Allen, *A New Testament Commentary*, p. 364.

Chapter 9
[1] Nygren, *Commentary on Romans*, p. 415.
[2] In Everett Gill, *A. T. Robertson* (New Yord: MacMillan, 1943), p. 179.
[3] Phillips, *Exploring Romans*, p. 181.
[4] R. G. Lee, *Bought by the Blood* (Grand Rapids: Zondervan, 1957), p. 114.
[5] Strong, *Systematic Theology*, p. 332.
[6] *The Wycliffe Bible Commentary* (Chicago: Moody Press, 1962), p. 1219.
[7] From Myra Shafner, *Quiet Hour* (Elgin: IL, David C. Cook Pub. Co.).
[8] Martin, in *The New Bible Commentary: Revised*, p. 1040.
[9] Barnhouse, *Romans*, IX, 61.
[10] Frederick Gill, *Charles Wesley: The First Methodist* (Nashville: Abingdon Press, 1964), p. 40.
[11] Barbara Bowen, *Strange Scriptures that Perplex the Western Mind* (Grand Rapids: Eerdmans, 1944), pp. 31, 32.
[12] F. W. Boreham, *The Silver Shadow* (London: Charles H. Kelly, 1918), p. 16.

Chapter 10
[1] J. W. Allen, in F. F. Bruce, *Romans*.
[2] Richard Wolff, *Riots in the Streets* (Wheaton, IL: Tyndale House, 1968), p. 130.
[3] Charles Ryrie, "The Christian and Civil Obedience," *Bibliotheca Sacra*, April, 1970, p. 157.
[4] John White, *Flirting with the World* (Wheaton, IL: Shaw Publishers, 1982), p. 97.
[5] Wolff, *Riots in the Streets*, p. 130.
[6] Bruce, *The New Bible Commentary: Revised*, p. 1163.
[7] Gifford, *The Epistle of St. Paul to the Romans*, p. 111.
[8] Henry Zecher, *Christianity Today*, 21 October, 1983.
[9] Roland Bainton, *Here I Stand* (Nashville: Abingdon Press, 1951), p. 244.
[10] Martin, *The New Bible Commentary: Revised*, p. 1041.
[11] Wolff, *Riots in the Streets*, p. 128.
[12] In Bruce, *Romans*, p. 234.
[13] Martin, in *The New Bible Commentary: Revised*, p. 1042.
[14] Robertson, *Word Pictures*, IV, 410.

Chapter 11

[1] Marlene LeFever, *Creative Teaching Methods* (Elgin, IL: David C. Cook Pub. Co., 1985), p. 155.

[2] John Knox, *The Interpreter's Bible, IX* (Nashville: Abinghdon Press, 1954), p. 614.

[3] Donald Cole, *Letters of Interest,* May, 1969.

[4] In *How to Give Away Your Faith* (Downers Grove, IL: InterVarsity, 1966), p. 99.

[5] Barclay, *Romans,* p. 181.

[6] James Engel, *Contemporary Christian Communications: Its Theory and Practice* (Nashville: Thomas Nelson, 1979), p. 223.

[7] Little, *How to Give Away Your Faith,* p. 96.

[8] McClain, *Romans,* p. 232.

[9] Bruce, *Romans,* p. 25.

Chapter 12

[1] Ralph martin, *New Testament Foundations, II* (Grand Rapids: Eerdmans, 1978), p. 188.

[2] From William Barclay, *Romans,* p. 199.

[3] Ibid., p. 203

[4] Martin, *The New Bible Commentary: Revised,* p. 46.

[5] According to Ernst Kasemann, *Romans,* p. 412.

[6] G. C. D. Howley, in J. B. Watson, ed., *The Church* (London: Pickering and Inglis, 1951), p. 113.

[7] *Christianity Today,* 5 October, 1979, p. 26.

[8] Edmond Hiebert *Personalities Around Paul* (Chicago: Moody Press, 1973), p. 201.

[9] Bruce Metzger, Princeton Theological Seminary class notes.

[10] Leon Morris, *The Apostolic Preaching of the Cross* (Grand Rapids: Eerdmans, 1956), p. 215.

[11] Robert Gundry, *Survey of the New Testament* (Grand Rapids: Zondervan, 1970), p. 278

[12] Ian Macpherson, *The Art of Illustrating Sermons* (Nashville: Abingdon Press, 1964), p. 54

DIRECTIONS FOR GROUP LEADERS

The questions and projects below should form the framework of the actual time spent in group discussion. The week before every class the leader ought to assign both the lesson and the Bible passage (found under each chapter title) to be read for the upcoming class so that students will come to class with an informational foundation for the discussion.

Some class members may come without having read the lesson for the week. It would be wise to have a plan for including them in a short review session before jumping into the study proper. Perhaps two or three other class members could give an "overview report" with highlights from the reading. Certain portions of the book could be read aloud. Or, you could set up a short dialogue session between two who have read the lesson content. However you do it, make sure the unprepared members feel every bit as important to the class as the others.

The New International Version, 1984 edition, is the Bible translation quoted throughout the commentary, although the study can be conducted using any helpful translation. Remember to read the directions for each chapter at least a week before class. That way, you will have adequate time to pull together some of the special learning experiences requiring advance preparation.

To encourage group discussion, don't be shy about asking, "Susan in what ways has this issue been a part of your own life experience?" If someone responds to a question, you can add something like, "How have others of you dealt with this?"

Don't be afraid of respectful disagreement, for we can learn from people who differ from us. Even if you don't agree, you can comment, "I don't think I agree, but it will certainly give us something to think about. How do others of you feel?" The secret of effective group discussion is to keep throwing open-ended questions (not questions that can be answered with a mere "yes" or "no") back to members of the group. Be sure to acknowledge people's contributions: "Thanks for sharing that, David. I know it took some courage to bring that up."

Try to include in all your group sessions some of the key ingredients

113

for building group life: a time for sharing, a time for prayer, and perhaps light refreshments around which significant conversation can take place. Bible study groups can be much more than just an intellectual trip. They can become a means of developing strong bonds of Christian fellowship.

Below, three items will be found for each of the 12 class sessions:

A. A Need-hook. Each week this paragraph will provide a discussion item with which to open class. Normally it will try to hook into some felt need humans experience that will in turn tie into a major truth emerging from the Bible passage to be studied. Hence, the leader moves the class from a felt need to the Bible principles.

B. Fun Feature(s). Every week the leader is provided with an activity (to do or discuss) with an element of group action or even humor involved. This group game or project will sensitize the students to an idea or issue from the particular passage being studied.

C. For Group Discussion. While there are usually a number of questions included within the body of the commentary at pertinent points in the flow of the study, seven to ten extra application questions on each given Bible passage are supplied here. The leader should allow plenty of time for students to think about and respond to the questions. If all questions and activities are used, the class time will probably take about an hour (although by selectivity in the use of the questions, the class time could be made shorter).

Happy study and good grouping to you!

CHAPTER 1

A. Need-hooks

1. Ask: "Have you ever felt out-of-kilter (physically, emotionally, careerwise, etc.)? Describe the situation. What brought about a righted situation?" From there move to the heart of Romans as presented in the overall outline.

2. Provide all small groups with a fairly small puzzle. Time them. Whoever gets the most pieces of the puzzle put together in the given time gets the prize. Romans tells us how God is putting the broken Humpty Dumpty of humanity back together again.

B. Fun Feature

1. Divide all students into pairs. In four minutes the pairs are to compare their own backgrounds, likes, and dislikes. Whichever pair finds the most items they share in common wins. Romans shows how God is putting humanity back together.

114

2. Play *Magnificent Obsession.* Ask each student to name some important items found in his or her attic or basement that an archaeologist from Jupiter in 2120 A.D. might uncover there and guess to be that person's master passion. (Keep the game light.) Move then to Paul's magnificent obsession in Romans 1:14-16.

C. For Group Discussion

1. In his opener, Paul found a way to include more than one type of person (refer to comments on "grace" and "peace"). In what way have you observed someone acting inclusively or making a very diversified group feel comfortable?

2. In what concrete way have you "received grace" (Rom. 1:5)?

3. What person do you think of as serving God with his or her whole heart (1:8)? Have you witnessed this?

4. What relationship do you see between planning and praying? Compare Romans 1:10 in context.

5. When and how have you been "mutually encouraged" (1:12)?

6. How, from Romans 1, do you answer the age-old question: "How can people be lost who have never heard about Christ?"

7. What powerful effects of the Christian Gospel have you observed (cf. 1:16)?

8. Can you give a living illustration of how sin brings people down in its downward spiral?

9. See if you can list the first 20 sins that come to mind committed by people today? How does your list compare with that in Romans 1:29-31?

10. What are three illustrated ways people can be "senseless, faithless, heartless, [or] ruthless" (Rom. 1:31)?

CHAPTER 2

A. Need-hooks

1. Ask: "What examples of religious hypocrisy can you recall from newspaper headlines and TV accounts over the past ten years?" Link this discussion with Romans 2:19-24.

2. Bernard Ramm (*Protestant Biblical Interpretation,* p. 75) says that sometimes "the scholar stuffs his academic britches with . . . commentaries and thus the Bible as God's word never reaches his soul." What are some things Christians use as "britches" padding to insulate themselves against integrity?

B. Fun Features

1. Let students discuss behavior standards (rules, politeness, "don't dos") in their home upbringing. See if they can name a parental rule that was unrealistic or soon outgrown. Then move to discuss the in-built moral standards of Romans 2:14, 15 that reveal themselves in conscience.

2. Let students name as many questionable badges, symbols, earmarks, etc. of spirituality, being Spirit-filled, being doctrinally okay, denominational acceptableness, etc., as they can. Then turn to how the ancient Jews used circumcision as their comfortable badge of okayness.

C. For Group Discussion

1. Can you think of an example of how you caught yourself doing something you'd criticized someone else for (Rom. 2:1, 3)?

2. How would you answer someone who quotes Romans 2:7 to argue that if you just do the best you can morally, God must reward you with eternal life?

3. Can you give an example of how "God does not show favoritism" (Rom. 2:11)?

4. What do you think the "conscience" is (Rom. 2:15)? Was Jiminy Cricket's adage correct: "Let your conscience be your guide"?

5. How would you update Romans 2:17 to your own religious setting?

6. What would you say to someone who says that Romans 2:17-24 is an example of Christian anti-Semitism?

7. What are some externals that modern religious people unwittingly come to trust in (cp. Rom. 2:25-29)?

8. In Romans 3:1-8 Paul tackles four tough questions skeptics raised. What do you think are five tough questions modern skeptics raise? What insights provide at least partial answers to these questions?

9. If someone asked you, "What advantage is there in being a Christian?" (paralleling Rom. 3:1), how would you reply?

CHAPTER 3

A. Need-hooks

1. Ask class members if they can recall any occasion when they felt totally hopeless, helpless, or abandoned. After they've shared, relate this helplessness and hopelessness (Eph. 2:12) to the dire diagnosis of Romans 3:10-20.

2. Ask class members to share instances of courtroom cases when they have served on juries. Tie these courtroom scenes in with the World Court scene of Romans 3:19-26.

B. Fun Feature

Play the Fun -tion [shun] Game. Give the class (divided up into teams of 5) no more than one minute to list in their groups as many of the Bible's -tions (that we shouldn't shun) as they can (e.g., salvation, justification, propitiation, etc.). After the race, hand out five wacky prizes to the winning team. Then see if the whole group can supply one-sentence definitions for each of the Bible's -tion terms.

C. For Group Discussion

1. How do you explain your "nice religious neighbor" in light of Romans 3:10-18?

2. Was there any particular sin that strongly sensitized you to your need of Christ?

3. Can you think of an occasion when you felt dumbfounded or dumbstruck (cp. 3:19)? How is sin a silencer?

4. Can you recall a vivid illustration of human wrong and guilt from literature or TV?

5. Can you recall an example of someone (from acquaintance or reading) who tried to make amends for sin in the wrong fashion?

6. What psychological benefits can you name that came from salvation being received by saving grace rather than being achieved by self-efforts?

7. Can you suggest a personal illustration of God's "forbearance" (3:25)?

8. Have you ever received money as a gift (cp. 4:4)? How did that feel in contrast to a regular salary?

9. If you wanted to argue that Romans 4:5 permits all kinds of immoral permissiveness, how would you argue?

10. If you had to draw a picture representing your forgiveness, what would you draw (cp. 4:7, 8)?

CHAPTER 4

A. A Need-hook

Let groups of four students draw up lists as if they were sub-committees of the Cosmic Committee on Personal Evil. Let them pretend that Jesus never entered history for salvation. They must brainstorm conceivable ways to counter personal evil in our world.

Give the groups five minutes to brainstorm; then, let each group report how they might have imaginatively handled evil. After reports, move to God's actual method in Romans 5:12-21.

B. Fun Features

1. Pass out index cards and pencils. Each person is an ad agent, acting for Abraham, who has just received the information of 4:18, 19. Write up an amusing pre-birth announcement as an ad agent for the 100-year-old Abraham.

2. Let groups of three compose their own Eternal Life Insurance Benefits Policy, using formal sounding insurance language where possible. After each group reads its composed policy, relate these to the benefits detailed in 5:1-5.

C. For Group Discussion

1. How do you think Jewish circumcision (4:10-12) is like Christian baptism?

2. Romans 4:15 says that "law brings wrath." What early childhood memory of broken family rules helps you illustrate this verse?

3. What do you think is meant by 4:18—"Against all hope, Abraham in hope believed"?

4. Have you known any believer who "rejoice[d] in . . . sufferings" (5:3)? Please share the story.

5. In what specific way have you seen "perseverance [produce] character" (5:4)?

6. Can you think of an example from history or news where someone sacrificed himself for another person (5:7)?

7. What are some modern instances where you felt God has "demonstrate[d]" His love (5:8)?

8. In what arenas of life today can you give examples of "reconciliation" (5:10, 11) taking place?

9. What are some words or expressions you would use (e.g., "lavish," "generosity") to help convey the meaning of God's "grace" (5:15, 17)?

10. In what ways is Adam's sin like Christ's salvation? In what ways is Adam's sin unlike Christ's gift?

CHAPTER 5

A. A Need-hook

Let class members compile a list of various addictions that humans get hooked on. (Make the list relevant to church people, e.g., chocolate, potato chips, TV sports programs, praise from being on various church boards, etc.) Move then to the idea of sin-as-slavery in Romans 6:6, 16 ff.

B. Fun Features

1. Have someone come in dressed in a dentist's white coat, carrying an extra long needle. A second actor is the patient. Compose a brief (Laurel and Hardy type) script they can act out, revolving around the dentist explaining to the patient that she is being injected with SIN-NOVOCAINE, which will deaden her to sin. After the hilarity is over, move to the counterpart in Romans 6:11 ("dead to sin").

2. Give students (in groups of three) paper and pencil. Ask them to come up with some imaginary modern equivalent for the drama of baptism (Rom. 6:3, 4). For example, the dying and rising of a seed illustrates a similar idea.

C. For Group Discussion

1. What are some ways that people try to "live a new life" (Rom. 6:4) apart from Christ?

2. Baptism is a sort of dramatic reenactment of spiritual truth (6:3, 4). What other mini-dramas of Christian reality are there?

3. Do you think it's possible for a seemingly harmful habit (e.g., squeezing the toothpaste tube from the middle) to become a sin? Explain.

4. What are some sinful attitudes that church people may fall prey to?

5. Do you feel "freed from sin" (6:7)? Why do you think we Christians often don't feel that way?

6. Have you read or experienced any practical tips that help you "count yourselves dead to sin" (6:11)?

7. Can you think of someone who has used a part of their body (6:13) as an instrument for righteousness?

8. What motivation do you think grace has that law doesn't (6:15)?

9. Cite an example from newspaper or television report of someone who is a slave to sin (6:16).

10. What is one area of holiness (6:19) in which you sense personal spiritual growth?

CHAPTER 6

A. A Need-hook

George Bernard Shaw said, "The earth is a nursery in which men and women play at being . . . saints and sinners; but they are dragged down from their fool's paradise by their bodies." How true has this been in your acquaintance? Discuss helps for preserving purity.

B. Fun Features

1. Let students pretend each has a Sin Consultant. What three things would they want their Sin Consultant to do for them?
2. Let students see if they can recall some childhood incident when they were stimulated into doing something wrong by the very fact of being told not to do that thing.

C. For Group Discussion

1. Can you recall a time when you felt a sudden spree of freedom (e.g., the last day of classes in elementary school)? How do you see this freedom relating to Romans 7:2, 3?
2. Romans 7:4 likens Christianity to a marriage. How many parallels can you suggest between being a Christian and being married?
3. Can you remember a time before you were a Christian when you felt "controlled by the sinful nature" (7:5)? Share.
4. What is one way that you seek to "serve in the new way of the Spirit" (7:6)?
5. Give a specific example of how you have come to recognize or identify some particular sin in yourself through an awareness caused by God's written revelation (7:7, 13).
6. What is one personal example of a "covetous desire" (7:8)?
7. Did you ever feel that sin sprang out at you like a roused lion from sleep (7:9; see the illustration in the commentary section)?
8. Can you give an illustration from your experience of "I do not understand what I do" (7:15)?
9. What is one area of struggle that you, your child, or a friend have felt torn up over inside—like Paul in Romans 7:15, 16, 18, and 19?
10. Does any Bible verse come to mind from your experience when you think of "delight[ing] in God's law [or Word]" (7:22)?
11. Recall an occasion when you experienced some victory over sin (7:24, 25)? Share.

CHAPTER 7

A. Need-hooks

1. Let students in groups of three discuss one tension each feels between present struggles and future glory (Rom. 8:21-25).
2. Go around the room and let as many participants as will do so to

answer the question, "When have you ever felt like a walking paradox?" (For instance, as a child you might have won a spelling bee, but on the same day been chosen last for a volleyball game.) Relate the stories shared to the early Roman Christians who were "more than conquerors" (8:37) while (paradoxically) at the same time they were literally being treated "as sheep to be slaughtered" (8:36).

B. A Fun Feature

See if class members can recall some old comedy show where the characters involved (e.g., Laurel and Hardy, the "Kingfish") had gotten themselves into a pickle, but by the end of the show or story all things had worked out for the best (8:28). Then let students peruse Romans 8 in their Bibles in order to name as many ways as they can from that chapter that demonstrate the truth that all things work together for good for those who love God.

C. For Group Discussion

1. How do we know that "the flesh" (8:5-8, KJV) includes more than just physical sins?

2. How might the Spirit of God be compared to an uplifter, elevator, or airplane in Romans 8:2, 3, 9-11?

3. Do you think Romans 8:8 is an absolute statement without exceptions? On what do you base your answer?

4. What do you think it means to be "led by the Spirit of God" in the context of Romans 8:14? Does this coincide with popular uses of the phrase?

5. Share a time when God enabled you to overcome fear (8:15).

6. What are some real-life examples of "present sufferings" (8:18)?

7. How would you put Romans 8:26 and 27 into your own words or frame of reference?

8. On what occasion have you realized that God was working something "bad" out "for the good of those who love him" (8:28)?

9. What in Romans 8:29-39 gives you special assurance?

10. With what do you identify most in Romans 8:35-39?

CHAPTER 8

A. A Need-hook

Ask class members to recount a bewildering experience when they tried to figure out what God was doing. Relate this discussion to the mystifying mystery of God's working in regard to His chosen people in Romans 9—11 (see 11:1).

B. Fun Features

1. Take a puzzle that has already been put together. First, divide it up into the number of groups you want to have in your class (e.g., if eighteen students and three students per group, then divide your puzzle up into six sections). Keep all the pieces of each section together in their own group, but take all the pieces apart within each group. Pass out the torn-apart groups of puzzle to each group of students to put together. Even if a group of students gets its puzzle pieces together, it will still be puzzling, because they will have only their section of the total puzzle. Relate this to the puzzling purposes of God in Romans 9— of which we have only partial knowledge.

C. For Group Discussion

1. What are privileges Christians might list (cp. Rom. 9:3-5) over which they can get smug?
2. When have you felt like saying, "God is unjust"? (Cp. 9:14)
3. Do you believe God's will is unresistable (9:19)? Explain.
4. Who do you think of as a sterling example of a Christian intensely wanting others to be saved (10:1)?
5. In what ways can Christians concretely demonstrate that "there is no difference" (10:12) between believers of various racial, ethnic, political, or economic backgrounds?
6. How were you brought the Good News (10:15) about Christ? What are some effective and noneffective ways of conveying Christianity (using specific illustrations)?
7. How do you reconcile Romans 11:6 and James 2:24?
8. Can you think of a seemingly bad situation (11:11, 12) that brought about eventual good results?
9. A Jew was "talking to . . . Gentiles" in 11:13. What barriers are you aware of in presenting Christianity cross-culturally or to another race?
10. Can you give an example of the intermingling of "the kindness and sternness of God" (11:22)?
11. Why do you want to worship God after reading 11:33-36?

CHAPTER 9

A. A Need-hook

See if each student can come up with his or her own classic case of someone (at the office, a past church, etc.) difficult to get along with. Direct the discussion back to Romans 12-14—principles for the giving of ourselves and getting along in the Body of Christ. (Don't forget 12:18's "if" for those classic cases!)

B. Fun Features

1. Let students go through the list of gifts in Romans 12:6-8 and name at least one Christian they know who possesses each of those spiritual gifts.

2. Divide students into groups of four. Ask each group to use Romans 12:16a ("Live in harmony with one another") as the title of their latest book. Let each group come up with ten zany rules for harmonious living (e.g., "Only proceed out in public on sunless days" or "Throw car into reverse gear at 50 M.P.H. when you have a tailgater behind you"). After groups share their lists aloud, move to Paul's contrasting principles in 12:14-21.

C. For Group Discussion

1. In what way have you found giving your body over to God a "sacrifice" (12:1)?

2. How would you define "not [being] conform[ed] . . . to the pattern of this world" (12:2)? Does it mean not wearing dresses designed by a non-Christian company, or not listening to music less than thirty years old?

3. How do you think we "test and approve what God's will is" (12:2)?

4. Do you think it's possible to think of yourself more lowly than you ought to think (12:3)? Explain.

5. Can you tell about a specific way another Christian's spiritual gift (12:5-8) has benefited you?

6. Give an example of how someone has honored you (12:10).

7. What helps you "keep your spiritual fervor" (12:11) up?

8. Can you describe an instance of someone practicing hospitality (12:13)?

9. Recall a time when you practiced Romans 12:14 and 17a.

10. Without naming names or supplying giveaway clues, can you describe a case where you felt it was impossible to "live at peace" (12:18) with someone?

11. What is an example of overcoming "evil with good" (12:21)?

CHAPTER 10

A. A Need-hook

Pretend you live in America in the 1770s. What would be reasons pro and con for joining the fight of the colonies against England? Suppose you were a German Christian in 1940. What quandaries would you have faced if you had been summoned to serve under Hitler?

B. Fun Features

1. During the prior week, let two versatile class members plan a short debate for class. One should argue that we ought to keep every jot and tittle of the Old Testament Law. The other should play an amoral radical spouting "love" slogans. After the comedy is over, let the class comment on "love is the fulfillment of the law" (13:10).

2. Ask students: "What is your most memorable memory of waking up?" Let everyone who will do so share aloud. Then expand on the moral "wake up" call in 3:11.

C. For Group Discussion

1. Do you think Romans 13:1 covers all cases without exception in regard to civil government?

2. How might 13:1, 2 be abused by civil rulers?

3. What is one practical value you derive from 13:1-5? To what extent should Christians be involved in the political process?

4. Suppose you lived in the Capone era in Chicago and found that virtually all local government officials were bribed, how would you come to terms with 13:4?

5. Can you think of two ways within your own lifetime that some government official "is God's servant to do you good" (13:4)?

6. How would you describe a particular person you know who deserves honor (13:7)? Doesn't giving people honor make them proud?

7. In what ways is love like a tax (13:8)?

8. What person do you feel a love tax toward?

9. How do you relate love and the moral Law (13:8-10)?

10. Think of a particular instance where you were involved with "dissension and jealousy" (13:13). How did it arise? Is it always avoidable? What can be done to prevent these two sins?

CHAPTER 11

A. A Need-hook

Briefly share your understanding of the "weak" and "strong" Christian. Then let students in small groups come up with one case study each of a real-life situation where Romans 14's principles would come into play. Share and discuss.

B. Fun Features

1. You have invited a Christian over to dinner. He says, "I am offended (à la Rom. 14:21, KJV) that you have salt and sugar on your table. The Bible says our bodies are the Spirit's temple. Salt and sugar degenerate our bodies." What would you do?

2. Let each class member recall some situation where they felt some other Christian was engaging in a questionable activity or where someone else called something they were doing into question. Then let students come up with at least five principles out of Romans 14:1—15:6 that might furnish general guidelines for governing questionable matters.

C. For Group Discussion

1. What feelings do we tend to have (14:3) when some other Christian disagrees with something we do or hold?

2. Can you give a modern illustration of 14:5—one who "considers every day alike"?

3. What practical lesson does 14:6 teach us?

4. What is comforting and discomforting about 14:12?

5. What do you think is an example of "passing judgment on one another" (14:13)? What might be an example of putting a stumbling block in another's way (14:13)?

6. How do some people have a false view (or semi-gnostic view) of spirituality?

7. Who do you think of as a Christian who is "do[ing] what leads to peace and to mutual edification" (14:19)?

8. How might 14:21 be wrongly or excessively applied?

9. What is one passage of Scripture that has given you encouragement (15:4)?

10. What do you think is meant by unity (15:6)? How is unity different from uniformity?

CHAPTER 12

A. A Need-hook

Let students in small groups pick one of the following topics:
(1) low and high income;
(2) black and white;
(3) Chinese and Hispanic;
(4) Episcopalian and Pentecostal;
(5) male and female;
(6) a similar set of contrasts of their own choosing.

Each group is to pinpoint four areas that they think would generate points of tension between their chosen pair of opposites—even though these contrasting types of people are within the Body of Christ. After discussion of such differences, relate these problems to the Jew-Gentile problems of Romans 15:8-21.

B. A Fun Feature

Pass out paper and pencil. Following Paul's pattern of "Greet _____" in Romans 16:3-16, let each student:

(1) write out one complimentary note or prayerful wish for one other person in the class (make sure everyone is included); or

(2) pass out as many slips of paper to each student as there are students in class. Ask them to write some note of appreciation to every other individual who has been part of the class.

C. For Group Discussion

1. Can you think of an example of building a relational bridge to someone quite different from yourself?

2. Have you ever had a change of plans (15:22; cf. 1:13) that you had to explain at some length?

3. What is one form of giving to the poor (15:26) you've witnessed?

4. Do you recall an occasion when you felt you could be, or had been, a blessing to someone (15:29)? Share.

5. What modern application do you make of the fact that Paul mentions at least ten women in 16:1-16?

6. Can you think of someone who risked his or her life for another (16:4)?

7. Of what Christian might you say that he or she "worked very hard for you" (16:6)?

8. Who would you describe as "tested and approved" (16:10)?

9. Have you had any surrogate of whom you might say spiritually that she/he "has been a mother [or father] to me" (16:13)?

10. Can you think of any modern equivalents to Erastus (16:23 or 24)?

11. Compose your own mini-doxology (cf. 16:25-27) to the Lord in light of this particular class.